REAL LIFE STORIES
of J.C. and The Breakfast Club
...or 20 Minutes in the Dark with Madonna

by J.C. Corcoran

ISBN 1-891442-13-9

Virginia Publishing Co.
4814 Washington, #120
St. Louis, MO 63108
(314) 367-6612
www.wordnews.com

Dedicated to Dad,
who gave me the best
possible gift:
His time.

Foreword

J.C. Corcoran is not a jerk.

I offer this bit of faint praise right off the top because a lot of people think he's a jerk and because I know he's not.

Yet I'm not exactly startled when I hear the epithet attached to his name. As Corcoran himself has argued with numbing frequency, too many people base their opinions of him on negative things they've read in the press and on the snipings of self-promoting adversaries and self-styled protectors of public morality.

His occasional on-air screeds on this subject, often labeled "an address to the nation," generally have been broadcast in the wake of a news story or opinion column about him that has had the great misfortune to contain a factual error or four—which is to say, many of them.

Corcoran insists with some justification that people tend to reach different conclusions about him when their opinions are based on what they've heard with their own ears coming from the radio speakers in their cars, trucks, minivans, and SUVs on their way to work, home, and school since 1984 when he began working in St. Louis.

The book you hold in your hand, obviously, is not a J.C. Corcoran radio show coming out of the speakers in your car. But it reads very much like his shows sound: quick, punchy, funny, snarky, shamelessly name-dropping, full of tangents that miraculously work their way back around to the original topics, and full of himself.

Notwithstanding a few early chapters on family background, childhood victories and traumas and adolescent epiphanies—my favorite parts of the book, actually, because a lot of the details were new to me—this is a professional memoir. It's a backstage and on-stage account of a sometimes triumphant, sometimes calamitous career in American commercial radio that happens to coincide with a period of radical and dispiriting change in what used to be our most intimate and exciting electronic medium.

It should go without saying that these are Corcoran's stories, no one else's. They are the facts as he remembers them, motivations as he interprets them, the truth as he honestly believes it to be.

That's not to say others might not recall or construe things differently; but their opposing viewpoints are not represented here. Let them write their own damned memoirs.

Corcoran's detractors will hate this book upon publication, of course. They will ignore its breezy readability in favor of ridiculing its unsophisticated rhetorical style. They will dismiss its sometimes fascinating, always interesting and unabashedly self-serving content as further confirmation of the author's overbearing ego.

What a crock. Any memoir ever written was written by someone who believed his or her life was worth writing about; in other words, from someone with a fatter-than-average ego.

Still, the knee-jerk naysayers are entitled to their opinions, and they're entitled to express them for public consumption. A columnist and critic for the last twenty-one years, I'd be the last person in the world to suggest otherwise.

It would be nice, though, to see some fair criticism of this book, favorable or unfavorable, and that could happen. But I've seen enough inaccurate, distorted and specious reporting and commentary about Corcoran over the past sixteen years to dampen my expectations.

Readers who were too young to notice or who weren't paying attention sixteen years ago may not fully appreciate how fast and how much of an impact Corcoran had when he arrived in St. Louis in 1984. I was writing a column about radio and television for the *St. Louis Post-Dispatch* at the time, and I only had to hear Corcoran on the air once to know that things were going to change.

The truth is, we were overdue for change. St. Louis radio was in a complacent snooze before Corcoran blew into town. KMOX, the CBS-owned AM station under the autocratic control of Robert F. Hyland Jr., was skimming some twenty-five percent of the radio business off the top, leaving the other thirty or so commercial stations to peck each other to death over the crumbs with an assortment of music formats.

A one-time broadcasting genius, Hyland's programming sense and instinct for talent had long since faded by 1984, but he used KMOX's hard-news image, its control of live sports, his connections to the corporate and political elite and an intimidating personal style to maintain power. Competitors cowered and treated him with a deference usually reserved for bishops.

Not Corcoran. Young, cocky, a masterful technician and unafraid to take risks, Corcoran created a morning show at KSHE-FM that sounded like nothing else on the air. It ran fast and felt improvisational. It was driven by a guerrilla mentality, and it recognized no sacred cows, least of all Hyland and his Bogey Club crowd.

Corcoran's approach was irreverent, often disrespectful and, in those days, sometimes genuinely distasteful. But if his humor was often sophomoric, his show was fresh, contemporary and, above all, entertaining.

Some facts under the heading of full disclosure:

For Corcoran's first three years in St. Louis, my relationship with him was an arm's-length, professional one. As a critic, I gave him credit when it was due and savaged him when it wasn't. As a reporter chasing any number of Corcoran-esque controversies, I got my facts straight. Caught off guard by this, Corcoran had no alternative but to respect my work.

In 1987, I dropped radio coverage from my assigned duties in order to concentrate exclusively on television. A few months later, I started contributing on-air segments about television to morning radio shows on KSD-FM and KUSA. A few months after that, KSD hired Corcoran to host its morning drive-time show, and he added me to his group of regular contributors. I've never written about his ventures into television.

Our professional relationship became collaborative, and a personal friendship evolved out of it. We're still friends and collaborators today, even though I now critique television for the *New York Daily News* and his show now airs on KLOU-FM.

I like J.C. because he's a fundamentally decent person with a big heart who is intriguingly and sometimes bafflingly complicated. I don't have time for jerks.

Eric Mink
October 2000

Introduction

C omedian Steve Martin used to say, "Comedy is not pretty." I have bad news. Comedy has an even uglier sister.

Radio has broken my heart. The business I revered as a child, young adult and novice broadcaster has gone sleazy, creepy and stupid. It's also provided me with indescribable thrills and has allowed me to live out my dreams. It is with that love/hate mentality I can't seem to overcome that I present this book.

If you're reading this right now you're probably either a fan of the show, some sick sense of curiosity has compelled you to drop the sixteen bucks, or you just hate my guts enough to want to know more about me. Regardless of what has brought us together, please understand how deeply I care about the projects I take on. Respect on that level is really all I ask. But I caution you, too. You may think you know me. Chances are you don't.

Let me launch a pre-emptive "scud" in the direction of the cynics who will attempt to pick this book apart. I save everything. And I mean everything. If it's been written or said about me in the past sixteen years, I have it. Boxes and boxes of news clippings, video-tape, letters, memos, faxes, e-mail, ratings and other material have been plowed through in researching this project.

I can be a very dangerous man sometimes.

Radio is supposed to be fun. In the late seventies, when I was in the early stages of building my career, Chris Rea, who sang "Fool if You Think It's Over," had a new album at the same time Dire Straits new release was out. At a station staff meeting I suggested we plan a "Dire-Rea" weekend. Everyone in the room busted a gut. Then, of course, we didn't do it.

You're about to hear a lot of stories like that. They're all real. Trust me. My imagination isn't developed enough for me to make up stuff this good.

We've reached the point where almost everyone is familiar enough with the business side of professional sports to understand the concept of salary caps, athletes playing out their options, contracts not being renewed and the like. Mark McGwire, Wayne Gretzky and Marshall Faulk, for example, have all been traded or switched teams, not because they didn't produce, but because of the *business* decisions management made above them. And though nearly each of those concepts also applies to the business side of radio, a lot of people, media included, have tried to pretend they don't. The next time you hear someone speaking dismissively about how J.C. Corcoran "gets fired all the time," hand them a copy of this book. Then watch their eyes widen.

My father likes to remind me that the higher up you are on the ladder, the more your butt is exposed. So right.

Glenn Frey of The Eagles once told Bob Costas on the "Later" program, "People who don't have any talent are scared to death of people who do." I think I could write an entire book based on that, single thought.

Instead, for now, I give you *Real Life Stories of J.C. and The Breakfast Club ... or ... Twenty Minutes in the dark with Madonna.*

Chapter 1

JANUARY 1982
Buffalo, New York

W*hat was I doing here?*
This particular part of western New York was just plain bleak.
Only a year ago I'd been working in Washington, D.C., a city vibrant, beautiful, and culturally alive. But the consultants insisted Buffalo was a necessary move for me; the equivalent of taking steps back in order to get a running start. For seven years I had been bouncing from small town to small town as a disc jockey, entertaining the idea that by getting into management, I would somehow legitimize my career. But after frustrating station stops in Omaha, as well as in the nation's capital, friends like Howard Stern and others in the industry convinced me that I should be doing what I loved most and did best: morning radio.

So what was I doing here?
While I pondered the question on this particular day in January, it was announced on the local news that the Buffalo unemployment rate had hit nineteen percent.

And did I mention it was snowing?

When I *really* thought about what I was doing in Buffalo, however, bits of verse would begin floating around in my brain. For instance, everything Billy Joel described in his song, "Allentown," could have been nicely attuned to the city of Buffalo. One didn't have to know much about economics to know that the term, "the Rustbelt," was not intended as a compliment. A line from Bob Seger's "Hollywood Nights" also resonated in my brain; you know, the one about "finding myself further and further away from my home." And when it came to thoughts of the city as a whole, I thought of actor and filmmaker Albert Brooks, who once said of San Antonio: "The city looked like it was constructed for the purpose of storing manure for the rest of the world."

What was I doing here?

And just when I'd be on the verge of giving myself a good answer, a "positive" upbeat answer, Dingus Day would flash across my brainwaves.

For those curious about Dingus Day and its effect on my attitude, let me tell you what it is, then you can decide if I'm making too big of a deal about it or not. Dingus Day is a yearly local celebration that takes place on the day after Easter. Single women get to swat eligible men on the legs and butt with pussy willows. Men get to return the gesture by throwing water on the women. This celebration, I might add, constitutes the lead story on Buffalo's eleven o'clock news.

Not only was my career meandering in Buffalo, but also the radio station where I had been sentenced to work. "97 Rock," a once-great broadcast facility, had also fallen upon hard times. I was brought in to produce a spark and to revive their morning show. Looking back after a year of my best efforts, two things could be said: 1) I was a hit with the audience and the hip half of the print media, having won several awards for "Best Buffalo Morning Radio Show" and, 2) I was in constant trouble with station management and community officials.

Things were reaching a head. And even though I was popular with the audience and most of the press, this popularity only seemed to irritate the station brass even more.

Letters from our Canadian friends just over the Niagara River were pouring in. They were not, to say the least, complimentary. Apparently the Canadians had had their fill of ribbing about the plethora of strip clubs and tourist traps, which make up pretty much their entire business district. The fine folks at a popular fast-food chain took exception to our characterizing the funeral service for their recently deceased founder as a "Mc Wake." The principal of a high school on the outskirts of town was angry because I didn't get the station van into their homecoming parade on time, even though I'd explained on the air he'd given me lousy directions. The Catholic archdiocese of Buffalo was threatening a boycott unless I retracted statements I'd made about having been beaten senseless in parochial school. And then there was Mayor Jimmy Griffin.

Now, believe it or not, you've probably seen hizzoner. In the opening sequence of the 1980s Dabney Coleman NBC sitcom, "Buffalo Bill," Mayor Griffin can be seen with the star of the show in a mock ribbon-cutting ceremony. And in the Burt Reynolds/Goldie Hawn romantic comedy, *Best Friends*, Griffin can be heard yelling, "You'll never get to play for the Sabres playing like that!" at a group of boys engaged in a street hockey game. Griffin looked, and especially sounded, like actor Dennis Franz, and Griffin believed in Buffalo. Forget the fact that Buffalo was ridiculed in the sitcom, or that the scenes from *Best Friends* depicted Buffalo as the depressing, arctic tundra that it was.

When director Barry Levinson needed a stadium that could pass for the late 1930s, he chose War Memorial Stadium in Buffalo to shoot the baseball scenes for the Robert Redford drama, *The Natural.* Long since abandoned by the Buffalo Bills of the NFL, I found it ironic that the set designers actually had to make *upgrades* to the stadium in order to depict it as one set in 1939. (As far as I know, Mayor Griffin wasn't able to weasel his way into the film.)

Again, Mayor Griffin could be heard extolling the virtues of his city as a Hollywood Mecca. That is, at least you could when he wasn't yelling about **me**. The mayor had obviously had it with this radio guy, and wrote a letter to my boss at the station. On January 23, 1983, I received a memo from 97 Rock's general manager. It said:

"We have offended all Catholics. We have offended all Canadians. We have offended many sponsors. We have offended the mayor. This has to stop. From now on all commentary should be positive."

I unsuccessfully argued that the Canadian audience was not part of our ratings survey area, so what they thought about us was inconsequential. I unsuccessfully argued that McDonalds wasn't even one of our sponsors, so what right did they have to complain? I unsuccessfully argued that bashing a high school principal probably did nothing more than make me all the more popular with the kids who, incidentally, made up a sizable chunk of our target demographic. And I unsuccessfully argued that by being a Catholic myself, I could say things a non-Catholic couldn't.

The sum total of these unsuccessful arguments was very simple: Adhere to the memo and "be positive."

The next morning on the air, I commented that I was *positive* the two feet of snow being forecast would bring in more tourists.

At ten o'clock I pulled off my headphones, tossed them on my desk, and headed for the men's room. As I stood at the urinal I heard the bathroom door open, and immediately felt the presence of another person directly behind me. The voice of the general manager boomed off the tile walls of the cavernous room. "That's gonna be it, okay?" Two thoughts crossed my mind: 1) If I whirl around as though I'm in a state of total disbelief, I might just get away with urinating all over this guy's leg, and 2) Even though I had just been fired, this was going to make a great story some day.

What was I doing was here?

I was leaving.

And heading home.

"I think what makes us survive is what we call the great middle class. These workers with their common sense who just seem to know what's right and what's wrong. They mow their lawn and they shovel their sidewalk. They keep things going."
—Cartoonist Charles Schultz

Chapter 2

A friend of mine, critic Gene Siskel, once observed that one of the endearing things about *The Three Stooges* was that, regardless of where they were, they never seemed to belong. And we've all seen enough daytime talk shows to know that kids who seem to have difficulty fitting in, eventually fall into some form of show business.

I was an Irish kid growing up in the overwhelmingly Polish, lower-middle class southwestern section of Chicago, Illinois. As if that wasn't bad enough, I lived in a city divided in half over its baseball teams: with White Sox fans on the south side, and Chicago Cub fans on the north side. I, of course, was a Cub fan living on the wrong side of town. From 1958 through 1964 my uncle, Don Elston, was a relief pitcher for the Cubs. I spent my first four years in St. Camillus School fighting with kids who accused me of lying about that fact. I got my first lesson in rhetoric when, upon producing proof that I, indeed, had an uncle playing in the major leagues, the kids simply shifted into calling him a "bum." (You may recall the Cubs having had what some might call a poor millennium, and the sixties were particularly lackluster.)

My father took me to one weekend game each homestand at Wrigley Field, and because the tickets came from Uncle Don, we got to sit directly behind the Cubs dugout along the third-base line. It was an early introduction to the concept of the kind of "privilege" that comes with being, or just knowing, a celebrity. Although I had my favorite players (like Ernie Banks), I was an even bigger fan of the Cubs' broadcasters. Jack Brickhouse was the voice of the Cubs on WGN-TV. Never to be mistaken for Cary Grant, Brickhouse was a portly, bald, but extremely personable man who, I concluded, had the best job in the world. When I was about six, I bothered my father to bother my uncle to bother Mr. Brickhouse for a face-to-face meeting. Now, one of the interesting things about little kids is that they don't filter anything they say. So when I finally met him one June day as he was heading up the ramp to his broadcast booth perched above home plate, I squeaked, "Hello, Mr. Brickhouse. When I grow up, I'm going to get a job like yours and a haircut like yours." Half-heartedly attempting to camouflage his embarrassment, he bent over slightly, shook my hand and with an uncharacteristically wise look on his face, responded, "When you grow up, get a job like your father's and a haircut like your father's."

Of course, it wasn't until years later that I understood he'd been warning me that the world of broadcasting might not be everything I had assumed it would be. That day, all I knew was that I had met my idol, and he had the greatest job in the world.

I spent the next few years pestering other Chicago television personalities. A sort of "Cronkite-ish"-looking man named P.J. Hoff, a weatherman on WBBM-TV, was another favorite of mine. Hoff was also a cartoonist, and he incorporated characters like "The Vice-President of Looking Out the Window" (animated by tugging on hidden fishing line) into his forecast maps. He was kind enough to allow my dad and me to watch him do his segment from the studio one evening.

My parents' radio never moved off the 720 spot on the AM dial, WGN. It was, and still is, a full-service, news, talk and information station. Wally Phillips, the longtime morning man, did a special show each opening day of the baseball season, complete with interviews, sound bites and special songs and stories. (Sound familiar?)

Since our house was a short bicycle ride to Midway Airport, I would occasionally watch the WGN traffic-'copter land on summer evenings, and even managed to meet "Flying Officer Leonard Baldy," who was killed in a helicopter crash the following year.

A distinguished-looking young gentleman named John Drury had just arrived in Chicago and was anchoring the news on WBBM-TV. For a third grade class project, Drury was kind enough to answer my request for an interview. As we sat in the station's tiny lunchroom, I can still recall his advice: "You have to know a lot of things about a lot of things to be in broadcasting," he told me. Although I may not have always done such a good job at putting his words into practice, I never forgot that piece of advice.

In the meantime, a metamorphosis was taking place on the Chicago radio airwaves. Mainstay programs such as "The Big 89 Barn Dance" on 50,000 watt, clear-channel WLS were replaced by disc jockeys like Art Roberts, Bernie Allen and Clark Webber, along with something called the "Top 40." My sister, Nancy, five years my senior, was hitting her mid-teens at about the time The Beatles were setting foot on American soil. She had the radio on constantly, and my attention now shifted toward what was, arguably, some of the best on-air talent in the country on WLS.

When I wasn't attempting to chase down unsuspecting broadcasters, my summers were spent playing baseball. Our community participated in an extremely organized league in which the parents of every boy who passed a rigid try-out and was picked for placement on a team, had to accumulate "points" each year in order to qualify. Whether it was mowing the outfield grass at our private field, laying down the foul lines before games, attending meetings or working in the two-story brick concession stand behind home plate, the fathers *and* mothers had to participate, or you were dropped from the league.

None of the nonsense that seems to have permeated organized kids' sports today existed back then. Only players from the first-place team got a trophy at the year-end banquet, and there was no rule requiring that each child play in each game. At least, that's how it was until the rule was challenged at the league meeting one winter. But to understand this story, you have to know a little about my dad.

James F. Corcoran was born in Chicago in 1922. He attended Tilden Technical High School, was vice-president of his senior class and was very well liked. Dad told me he knew the name of every kid in his class, about 400-500 boys. Academically he was an above-average student, but because of the Depression and World War II, there wasn't any money to send him to college. One night, a day or two after he had graduated and was about to begin looking for full-time work, Grandpa Corcoran woke him up in the middle of the night. It seems Grandpa had gone to the racetrack (and had a few under his belt) and won the daily double. Grandpa asked Dad if he still wanted to go to college. The next day, Grandpa enrolled him in school, and Dad started classes almost immediately at Illinois Institute of Technology.

During his junior year in college, someone tipped Dad off that he was about to be drafted, presumably into the Army. Before the draft notice got to the house, he went down and enlisted in the Army Air Corp (later to become the US Air Force). Grandma cried that evening.

Late in his tour of duty he was granted a weekend pass, rendezvoused with his fiancee, Marjorie, here in St. Louis, and got married. After the war, he returned to my mother in Chicago and took a job as a mechanical draftsman.

Dad considered returning to college to get his degree, but five years had elapsed, and engineering had changed considerably. Also, with working full time and newly married, night school would have been a strain on both the budget and my parents' relationship. A few years later my sister came along, and Dad permanently shelved the hope of getting his degree.

My dad coached or managed nearly every year of the eleven years I played organized ball. With a little help from Uncle Don, and armed with an almost sick obsession for pitching (I often spent hours a day throwing), I developed into one of the better pitchers on Chicago's entire southwest side. It was not uncommon for me to strike out as many as eight or ten kids a game. But not every player on our team displayed the same level of intensity for the sport. After all, it was the sixties, and other interests were vying for our attention; namely, girls, cars and the time-honored tradition of just causing trouble. (In fact, a handful of the guys I'd been hanging out with would soon end up in jail, in reform school, or dead.) The league we played in took up as many as five nights or afternoons a week, and some of the players had one foot in and one foot out. And the league rule stated: If you missed practice, you couldn't play in the upcoming game.

My dad was always the quintessential "nice guy." He never swore and rarely drank. He was an honest, hard-working Democrat, dedicated to his wife and his family. He loved baseball and a good, clean joke. He was on cordial terms with most people, and he was very good with kids, especially boys.

I never got the idea that he derived much satisfaction from his chosen career field. Because he was always the "nice guy," with an aversion to making waves, I think this allowed his employer to take advantage of his good nature. Even today, I strongly believe that he was never paid what he was worth, promoted fairly, or recognized for his invaluable contributions to the company.

Maybe this failure to make waves at work had something to do with why he was so effective at coaching boys' baseball. And maybe that's why he stood up and spoke out on a cold, Chicago winter night at the league meeting.

One league official had the bright idea to institute a new rule requiring all managers and coaches to play every boy on every team in every game. One after another the league's brass took the podium in an overly pious parade which, clearly, had been orchestrated ahead of time. Nodding heads bobbed on the dais and in the crowd as the new league policy seemed headed for passage. The last thing anyone expected was for Jim Corcoran to get up.

He reminded the crowd of his years of coaching, briefly recounted some of his experiences, and then ripped into the proposed policy change.

"To play well, to play competitively, and to have any of this do any good for any of these boys, they have to *practice*. If you don't practice, you don't play. That's always been the rule. Unless I can tell a boy he's got to hustle in practice to be able to play in the game, I can't do my job as a manager," he said. Then (it's not exactly clear) he either threatened to stop managing, or just hinted that he might, and returned to his seat.

Clearly put back on their heels, the league officials made one last attempt at making a case for the rule change, claiming it was really "in the best interests of the boys." But now there were few nodding heads in evidence. The vote was taken. The rule change was defeated.

Our teams, coached or managed by Dad, went on to good, even great, record years. When I was fifteen, my final year in Babe Ruth League, I was selected as the starting pitcher for the Clear Ridge all-star tournament team. We won our first five games in the single-elimination competition. Winning the sixth meant we would travel to Olney, Illinois, for the state regionals. Now, when you're a boy in your middle teens, the very concept of **traveling** … on a real **team bus** … can be enough to keep you awake for a week.

In July of 1969, our team arrived in the far-south Chicago suburb of Mt. Greenwood to take on their all-star team. Their home field was much nicer than what we were accustomed to playing on. Their team had much bigger kids, too. Streamers, banners and tournament bunting adorned the facility as a crowd of roughly 2,000 spectators gathered. Our managers and coaches, in a surprise move, decided to throw lefty Kevin Porter instead of me. The strategy, I'd later learn, was to have Kevin lob up his enormous curveball against a potent Mt. Greenwood line-up for three or four innings, then have me come in and sail in my blistering fastball to throw off Greenwood's timing.

Our opposition scored twice in the early innings. I was brought in to relieve in the third. With the score still 2-0, I took the mound for my warm-up tosses before the fifth inning began. Suddenly, the public address announcer's voice came booming over the loudspeaker system with a definite tone of urgency.

"Ladies and gentlemen, may I have your complete and undivided attention? I have a very important announcement to make."

The huge crowd went—almost eerily—dead silent.

"I've just been informed that The United States of America has just successfully landed a man on the moon."

The crowd went wild. I took a bow.

We lost the game 2-1, ending up on the wrong end of a one-hitter. But on that momentous night, everyone cheered as Neil Armstrong took man's first step onto the lunar surface.

I played three more years of organized summer baseball, and added a spring schedule of games playing for my high school team. As a senior I played under Coach Schwarz, the school's basketball coach. Coach Schwarz heavily favored his beloved basketball stars, and somehow his players "mysteriously" managed to make the baseball team. After a particularly miserable performance against a lesser squad from Hales Franciscan, Coach Schwarz sat us down for yet another one of his convoluted tongue-lashings. He complained we were not playing "like a team," concluding, "That's why we're 4 and 4 instead of 10 and 0!"

That may have been the day I seriously began questioning authority.

Twice during that year, professional scouts were in attendance of games I pitched. A Padres scout watched me strike out nine, and a Giants scout witnessed an eleven strike-out game. But I never heard from either of the clubs. I finally had to accept the idea I was just not big enough to be taken seriously as an athlete, and shifted all my attention to broadcasting.

I had heard that WLS had a viewing room where you could watch the broadcaster while he was on the air. I got the chance to see Tom Lee, an enormous man who must have tipped the scales in excess of 350 pounds, cue his engineer for the song, "Tighter and Tighter" by "Alive and Kickin'."

The broadcasting bug had bitten.

Postscript: *In the economically challenged mid-1970s, the company Dad worked for went out of business, and after twenty years with the company, he was out of work for the first time in his life. Although Dad landed a new job later that same year, I think the experience permanently affected me. I knew he had worked as hard as anyone had in that company. He played the game right, but still lost. It was a lesson that would account for many of my career decisions and business dealings years later. But I also remembered his speech at the baseball league meeting, and it taught me that what you say and how you say it can make a difference. Especially when you know what you're saying is right.*

"I went to a tough school. The teacher asked, 'What comes after a sentence?' A kid raised his hand and said, 'You make an appeal!"

—Actor/Comedian Rodney Dangerfield

Chapter 3

Paul McMurray was my best friend and the smartest kid in the school. By the time we reached seventh grade, we had decided we were tired of apologizing for being two of only a handful of Irish kids in a school full of Polish kids. Both of us had already put up an enormous stink when the nuns tried to make us learn to sing Christmas carols in Polish. St. Patrick's Day was coming up, and I was still worked up about something that had happened to my older sister on that day several years earlier.

My mother had dropped off a batch of cupcakes adorned with shamrocks and green icing for my sister's class. A few hours later, Mom caught the nuns trying to sell them to the students during lunch.

Another incident occurred when my sister was in the fourth grade. The entire family could hear her wails from several blocks away as she neared our house. Some kid at school had been making fun of her name all day, twisting it into things like "cork head" and "popcorn." After my father had calmed her down and gotten the tears to stop, he asked which kid was responsible for teasing her like this. She answered, "Linda Czybowobiscz."

Since Paul came from a broken home, we had the run of his mom's townhouse while she was at work. We began planning our own St. Patrick's Day celebration for the school weeks before the big day. Soon Paul's basement began to look like the closing scenes of *Animal House* (remember the students' plot to take over the town parade?). And on this particular St. Patrick's Day, the students and faculty of St. Camillus School would arrive to find the halls and classrooms decorated with hundreds of shamrocks cut from construction paper, along with green and white banners, ribbons and assorted paraphernalia.

But it was the 75-foot-high light pole, which stood directly outside the school in full view of virtually all the classrooms, that was Ground Zero for us. Paul and I had sent away for three enormous, bright green weather balloons and filled them helium. Then we carefully tied them together with string, and looped the configuration loosely around the base of the pole. As soon as we let go, the balloons shot to the top of the pole, caught on the rim of the light and bobbed around in the wind. We theorized that the only way the school janitor would be able to get them down would be to *shoot* them down.

School ended early for Paul and me that day.

I think the St. Patrick's stunt was part of the reason I was sent to an all-boy Catholic high school run by the Christian Brothers, which I believed was one notch short of military school. One of the brothers confidently promised my parents they'd "make a man" out of me. They should have just said they intended to beat me into submission. (No lawsuits back in those days!) I should also mention, to validate my "brutal methods" claim, that one of the school's *appointed* positions was "Dean of Discipline."

One particular day, I lodged a terribly misguided protest over an algebra grade to Brother Regan, a red-faced, white-haired, stocky Irish immigrant whose breath occasionally hinted of alcohol. He liked to talk a lot about Knute Rockne, and in between football anecdotes, would offer blurringly-quick instruction of quadratic equations and other stuff (of which I never was a particularly good student).

As class was about to begin, I approached his lectern with report card in hand. I complained that the "D" he had given me should actually have been an "C." He argued it should have been an "F." He sent me back to my seat, whereupon, I evidently mumbled the wrong thing.

Now, this particular order of brothers seemed to take sadistic glee in knowing that we, as students, were fully aware of each instructor's— occasionally legendary—method of doling out punishment. It ranged from one brother's truckload of demerits for even a simple, disciplinary infraction to another who wielded a fraternity paddle when he didn't think an unruly student had gotten the point. Brother Regan, however, kept a slab of "neolite" in the top drawer of his desk. (Neolite was a sort of plastic/synthetic leather combination that was used to make shoe soles.) Where he had obtained this uncut, unprocessed chunk of matter, and how he arrived at this being his chosen implement of destruction, will always be a mystery. But how he used it, wasn't.

He liked to call the offending student to the front of the class, at which point he would instruct the victim to grab his ankles. Then he'd whack him on the ass with a level of intensity he felt matched the infraction. On this fateful "D" versus "F" day, he called me up to the front. But when he said, "Grab your ankles," I acted as though I didn't understand the instructions. I remained upright, lifting my ankle high enough to grab it with my hand. The next thing I remember was feeling pain and seeing stars. He beat me all over—head, shoulders, arms and legs—with this wedge of shoe sole material for what seemed like an eternity. I was still shaking three hours later when I got on the bus to go home. Even though I knew I had pushed the smart-ass thing too far, I also knew that he had gone entirely too far with the punishment.

When I got to school the next morning, I learned Brother Regan had had a heart attack and died during the night. It is an indescribable feeling to be barely fifteen years old and be in that much trouble. As I approached his casket at the wake, the eyes of every kid, teacher and administrator in the school were on me. I remember how sad and how unnecessary were the events leading up to this man's death.

Even though some higher-ups blamed me for Brother Regan's death, I wasn't expelled from school. Several factors were in my favor: My grades were good, I played several sports, and this was the first time I had been in trouble. More important, the other students in the class had given their account of the savage beating.

Instead, I was encouraged to channel my energy into something "positive." Since baseball only took up the last two and a half months of the school year, there was a lot of time that needed "positive" channelling. Luckily, there were a few unusually dedicated teachers who were willing to lend a hand in guiding me. One of the brothers noticed some etchings in my history notebook and put me in charge of the poster committee. Not *exactly* what I had had in mind, but it was a start.

During my junior year I noticed a kid from the Audio/Visual club recording the varsity basketball games with the school's new videotape machine. I heard the team would occasionally watch the tapes after practice, and I saw my chance.

After being granted a meeting with the assistant principal, I unveiled my plan to add my play-by-play to the tapes. I figured they could show the games during study halls, which might result in increased attendance. To my surprise, the administration bought it. The following week I was behind a microphone and, for the next two seasons, was the "Voice of the Vikings."

During a baseball game in the spring of my senior year, the thought occurred to me that a job at a microphone might even be a lot safer than playing ball.

Our main rivals were the "Crusaders" from Brother Rice High School. They were the "rich kids." (Actually, their fathers probably made about five thousand dollars a year more than our fathers, but in our minds that made them the rich kids.) Their school was in a much nicer part of Chicago's southern suburbs. Their field was more finely manicured. They had an indoor pool. They had much nicer cars. Their girlfriends were prettier. They usually beat us. We hated them.

We started our ace, Ray Jablonski, in the last game that we, as seniors, would ever play against our nemesis. I was not expected to see action that day, so I settled into a corner of the dugout, which provided me with a clear view of the students from Mother McCauley High School walking home from class. This was the all-girls' school situated directly across the street from Bother Rice, an institution that, years later, through the selective-breeding process, would produce a surgically altered product by the name of Jenny McCarthy.

"Jabbo," as he was known, had a tendency to fall off the mound to the first-base side following his ferocious delivery, which didn't put him in place to field his position very well. The last of the Mother McCauley girls had just passed by, and my attention was back on the game. I quickly wished I was still girl-watching. A left-handed hitter by the name of McFarlane laced a "Jabbo" fastball right back from where it had come. The loud crack of the ball shattering Jabbo's face was a sound that would take for me many years to forget.

It was nearly forty-five minutes before play could resume. Coach Schwarz told me to warm up and, quick as that, I was standing at the exact spot where our fallen warrior had stood moments before. This did not produce a secure feeling. But from that moment on, the mic in my hand, did.

Having just barely survived the system after four brutal years, there was one other incident of note that occurred just before graduation. Brother Lasik in addition to being the golf coach, was faculty advisor to the prom committee, of which I was a member. He had instituted one dumb policy after another, and was still upset that we'd booked a new band called "Rufus," which featured a young singer by the name of Chaka Khan to play at our homecoming sock hop the previous fall. We wanted to book another new band, "Mason Proffit," for the prom, but Brother Lasik was insisting on the "New Colony Six."

About two hours after dismissal from school one afternoon, Brother Lasik and I got into it about the bookings. Finally, he said, "All right, all right. Let's talk about this privately." I got up and walked with him about thirty feet down the hall, away from the other committee members. Without warning, he flew into a rage and began pounding me with a closed fist. My mind flashed back to Brother Regan and time stopped once again. It turns out the guys were peering around the corner and had seen the whole thing. Some of them told me they would have hit back if they had been in my shoes. I was especially relieved the next day when I saw that Brother Lasik hadn't had a heart attack or died during the night.

Postscript: *My date, Sue Cray, and I danced to the music of the "New Colony Six" on prom night. Our graduation ceremony was held at Medinah Temple in Chicago's "Loop." I felt lucky to have come out of the all-boy Catholic high school experience alive. Under James Corcoran in the senior yearbook was listed: Chairman of the Poster Club; Baseball 2, 3 and 4; Voted "Most School Spirit" and "Best Speaker."*

"I never worry about the future. It comes soon enough."
—Physicist Albert Einstein

Chapter 4

Those tapes from two years of calling high school basketball play-by-play got my foot in the door of the college radio station at Northern Illinois University in DeKalb. I had actually enrolled at SIU in Carbondale, but switched to Northern at the last minute when it dawned on me how cut off I would have been from the Chicago sports scene, my friends who had chosen to go to local colleges, and my girlfriend.

For the next four years I would volunteer for every assignment the two college radio stations offered. I became the first freshman ever to host a regular show on WKDI, the student-operated station that was piped into dorms and other campus buildings. I lobbied hard for a chance to become involved in the station's coverage of sports and, one weekend when one of the upperclassmen was faced with a scheduling conflict, I found myself heading to Carbondale, Illinois, to provide the color commentary for an NIU-SIU basketball game.

I must have done a decent job because the next few years took me to such booming metropolises—Fresno, California; Toledo, Ohio; Terre Haute, Indiana; and Mount Pleasant, Michigan—to call the play-by-play of NIU's basketball and football games. I distinctly recall one harrowing trip into the Blacksburg, Virginia, airstrip where the Marshall University football team had crashed just two years earlier.

We were doing such a good job that the other campus radio station, an NPR affiliate who actually broadcast over the air, decided to re-broadcast our play-by-play. Unfortunately, this was my first experience with what happens when you look like you're having too much fun. A drop-dead gorgeous talk show host from the station took me aside one day. I was convinced that my newfound "promotion" would result in her hitting on me. Instead—with great bitchiness, I might add—she wondered aloud whether I'd be able to do next week's game "without slandering anybody." It seems the previous week I'd referred to the NIU Marching Huskies as "trained lunatics." What she didn't know was that I was tight with the band, and they thought what I had said was hilarious. The Marching Huskies were even *grateful* for my comment—it was the first public acknowledgment they'd had that they even existed. But the message from on high was clear: The stuffed-shirts weren't liking us much.

It was a great time for sports fans and announcers in those days at NIU. The football team was being led by All-American fullback Mark Kellar, who had rushed for three thousand yards during his career at NIU. Our basketball team was being carried by an All-American candidate center named Jim Bradley. The team won twenty games my freshman year, and missed a bid to the NCAA tournament by an eyelash.

At an airport during a road-trip to Roanoke, Virginia, our sports information director asked my color man and I if we would mind sharing a rental car back to the hotel with an NBA scout. We thought that sounded cool, so we agreed. We ended up in the company of a cigar-chewing character by the name of Red Auerbach, the legendary Boston Celtics icon. (A potentially dangerous decision since the other DeKalb station's play-by-play guy, Russ Piggot, who had lost his right arm in a combine accident when he was a kid, insisted on driving. Even worse, Russ smoked, which meant he'd light his cigarette while steadying the steering wheel with his leg.)

Partially since DeKalb was situated in such a flat, low-lying part of the country, it was one of the first communities to be wired for cable. Few realize it, but in those days subscribers would hook up their stereo receivers to the cable, too, which allowed our tiny campus radio station to be heard throughout the region.

Today, DeKalb, Illinois, is best known for its patented corn seeds and as the hometown of model/actress Cindy Crawford. It is also the alma mater of *Back to the Future* and *Forrest Gump* director, Robert Zemeckis; an actress I fully expect will win an Oscar some day, Joan Allen; and the "Voice of Homer Simpson," Dan Castelenetta. But back then, the only thing we could hang our hats on about the place was the invention of barbed wire. (Later, a former DeKalb schoolgirl and actress named Cindy Morgan, would appear naked with Chevy Chase and Bill Murray in the comedy, *Caddyshack*.)

To stave off boredom, I attended as many "cultural" events, lectures and concerts as I could. Because of its proximity to Chicago's O'Hare Airport, NIU was able to attract an excellent array of guest speakers. In any given week you could see Ralph Nader, Gloria Steinem, the advertising executives who conceived Seven-UP's "Un-Cola" campaign, or a pair of young, network correspondents fresh from a trip to China by the names of Koppel and Donaldson. Author Saul Alinsky got my attention by insisting that any successful revolutionary became successful by working from the *inside*. I saw Elton John, The Beach Boys and B.B. King for the first time, as well as actors John Travolta and Marilu Henner in the touring company of *Grease*. I also saw my first foreign film.

Every six months I'd attend the latest revue at the Second City Improvisational Theater in Chicago's Olde Town. The young, unknown comedians and actors had names like George Wendt, Shelley Long, Bill Murray and John Belushi.

My parents paid for the biggest chunk of my school expenses, and I worked in factories each summer to make up the difference. My sister, who had worked in the bursar's office, told me about something called the "Talented Student Scholarship," which I promptly applied for, and was granted.

In May 1971, on the first anniversary of the Kent State tragedy, the campus got pretty much turned upside down. When students spilled into the streets, administration buildings were taken over and a curfew instituted, I got my first taste of live reporting and news-gathering under strained conditions. While there were some scary moments, I thought it was the coolest thing I'd ever done. From that point on, I signed up for as many journalism classes as I could afford to take.

You'll notice I haven't mentioned much about the actual curriculum at NIU. Yes, unfortunately, I have to confess that I was so interested in the opportunity to participate in outside activities, I degenerated into being just an average student. Most of it was my own fault, but the school wasn't helping. Case in point: my Television Production class was taught by a guy whose professional career consisted of having operated a camera at a Youngstown, Ohio, television station. (I did like my Radio Production class, however. The teacher's best broadcasting story was about the station manager who made him change his name because, if he said "Rod Diehl" too fast, it came out sounding like "raw deal.")

All in all, I didn't exactly feel challenged.

Until that is, the head of the department suggested a course of independent study. This meant I could run all over Chicago and north-central Illinois doing interviews and preparing documentaries on topics that interested me. I spent several fascinating days at the Center for UFO Studies in Evanston, Illinois, with Dr. J. Allen Hynek, the world's foremost authority on the subject. (Dr. Hynek's work served as an inspiration for Steven Spielberg's film *Close Encounters of the Third Kind*, which came out several years later.) I toured the Chicago radio market and interviewed two of my idols—Larry Lujack of WCFL and Bob Sirott of WLS. I was working full time at the campus radio station, and was on the air as much as four times a week. But WKDI's format was underground, progressive rock; I, on the other hand, was doing commercial, mass-appeal radio stuff, which many of the music purists despised.

The day before Thanksgiving break of my senior year, I was fired from WKDI for playing the sound-effect of a turkey during my show. It was just the kick in the head I needed. I had clearly outgrown college radio. A friend had told me about an opening at a tiny station about halfway between DeKalb and the northwest Chicago suburbs. I was hired the next week. Every afternoon I'd finish class around one, then drive forty miles through the back roads of Illinois farm-land to Dundee, where I hosted a five-hour show on WVFV. My pay was one hundred dollars a week.

Postscript: *I skipped my graduation ceremony since it fell on the same day as The Eagles/Dan Fogelberg concert in Chicago. My diploma came in the mail about a month later. I was ready to begin my professional broadcasting career.*

"Getting there is half the fun."

—Anonymous

Chapter 5

Whoever said, "Getting there is half the fun," should be shot.

With diploma in hand and a dumb-looking, naive grin on my face, I walked into WYFE radio in Rockford, Illinois. I had sent the program director, Mike Anderson, a tape and resume months ago, but an old pal from WKDI who was working the late-night shift there coaxed his boss into seeing me.

"I see here you're a college graduate," Anderson observed.

With that same dumb-looking, naive grin I responded, "Yes, sir!"

"Well, I never hire college graduates," he announced. On my way out, I noticed he had written something in the margin of my resume: "Bad voice."

A few weeks later I was sitting in a DeKalb bar with the same friend who'd gotten me in to see the WYFE program director. This friend had brought along an obnoxious buddy who, even though he had no background in broadcasting, felt compelled to share with me all the reasons I'd never make it in the business. I don't recall precisely what he said that made me throw that beer in his face but I remember thinking, as a bouncer deposited me on the curb, that it might make a good story someday.

A few days later Mike Anderson called and asked me to come into the station. When I got there, Anderson told me he knew the guy whose face I had pitched the beer in, hated him, and then offered me the all-night job.

I recall wondering if I'd just gotten a job for throwing a beer in a guy's face, but I didn't care. I took the job and, at approximately 3 a.m. one June morning in 1975, hit a button, and the Doobie Brothers' "Take Me in Your Arms," began playing. I was in business.

A few months later the afternoon guy got fired, and I got moved up. Then the morning girl quit, and I moved into that slot. About a year later, though, the station hired a new consultant, fired the program director and changed the format. I was quickly out of a job.

The old WYFE program director had moved onto an AM station in Flint, Michigan, and offered me the all-night show with the understanding that as soon as he could fire the morning guy, I'd be given the job. Now, anyone who's ever seen the Michael Moore film, *Roger and Me*, knows about Flint. I assure you it was much worse. I lasted three months.

I moved back in with my parents in Chicago. An old college radio friend had gotten a job at an also-ran FM station so, naturally, I began hanging around. I got hired to do weekends and, eventually, mornings when the program director who hired me got fired. A bunch of coked-out guys came in six months later, changed everything from the station's call-letters to the format, and my short-lived stint doing morning radio in my home town came to an abrupt end.

I was so disgusted by my experience that I decided to switch gears, by taking a huge step backward and starting over in Top 40 radio. There was an opening in Fort Wayne, Indiana, and I took it. From there I went to Lansing, Michigan, where I can recall only two interesting things to happen: my first encounter with the meteorological phenomenon "thunder snow"; and a guy by the name of "Magic," who led Michigan State University to a national basketball championship in 1979. A year later I was in Milwaukee, where I saw a young comic by the name of Jay Leno perform at the annual Summerfest event on the lakefront. I then followed a friend (and a job lead) to Omaha, Nebraska, where I interviewed Mickey Mantle, covered the college baseball World Series, and called the play-by-play of an Omaha Royals baseball game as part of a special broadcast during the Major League strike of 1981. I also anchored a pre-game show for Nebraska football on a twenty-two-station network. It was not uncommon for me to leave work on Friday, and not have a conversation with another human until my return to the station on Monday.

I was going nowhere fast and I knew it. I decided the only place I really wanted to be was back home in Chicago. I quit my $23,000 a year job, and moved back in with my parents. After six months and a half-dozen interviews that came up empty, I took a job with an old friend who was now running DC 101 in Washington. The station had a guy I'd been hearing a lot about—Howard Stern—doing mornings. I took the job and assumed the titles of promotion director, assistant to the program director, and weekend air talent.

Shortly after my arrival in D.C., Howard's contract negotiations broke down and he announced he'd be leaving for WNBC in New York. Robin Quivers, Fred Norris and the rest of Howard's gang sort of came and went, but Howard and I spent a fair amount of time talking about the business. He really encouraged me to get out of the management side and back on the air full-time. By the time Howard left D.C., there were about three people still talking to him. I was one of them.

Two, new jocks came in that summer. One I liked. One I didn't. Asher Benrubi, aka, "Adam Smasher" or "The Smash," was a real character with a big heart. We quickly became friends; a friendship that would be tested many years later. Doug Tracht, aka, "The Greaseman," was a redneck with some odd ideas about people whose skin color wasn't the same as his.

A consultant friend of mine convinced me I needed to take a step back in order to get a running start and return to doing what I loved most and did best: morning radio. In the midst of the Washington Redskins march to the Super Bowl I packed my things and headed for Buffalo, New York. The day I arrived in January of 1982, it was announced on the news that the metro unemployment rate had hit nineteen percent.

Did I mention it was snowing?

Oh, but you've heard that story before, haven't you?

> *"A consultant is a person who borrows your watch to tell you what time it is."*
>
> **—Newscaster Eric Sevareid**

Chapter 6

I'd sent out sixty-one tapes and resumes trying to get out of Buffalo and, obviously, wasn't having much success. Then I took a friend's suggestion, and began sending them to the consultants and "group" program directors that oversee entire radio station chains.

I didn't realize it at the time, but a real transformation was taking place in FM morning radio. Rock stations had traditionally focused the majority of their attention and resources on the afternoon, evening and nighttime shows. Morning radio had not been the place to be on an FM rock station.

However, disc jockeys like Howard Stern in Washington and Steve Dahl with Garry Meier in Chicago were starting to get the attention of the industry with completely unrestrained programming on their morning shows. But there was a great debate raging as to whether shows of this nature could ever prosper outside of big cities. Most observers insisted they could not.

In the late winter of 1984 I received a call from the group program director of Emmis Broadcasting, a relatively small company based out of Indianapolis, which had just taken over one station in Los Angeles and another in St. Louis. He said they'd listened to my tape and liked a lot of what I'd been doing in Buffalo, then asked me how I'd feel about working for their St. Louis station. Now, I was so sick of snow and so homesick for my family, National League baseball and the Midwest that, although I'd never set foot on Missouri soil, I began reeling off every scrap of St. Louis trivia I could think of.

I was on a plane to St. Louis later that week. But I was in for a big surprise when I got there.

Instead of meetings, discussions or schmoozing, KSHE's management team checked me into the Airport Marriott with the following instructions: "Listen to morning radio for the next three days. At the end of the three days, we're going to ask you this question: How do you think you'd do against Mark Klose?"

Mark Klose, of course, was the longtime, market veteran who had left KSHE after years of service, only to take his talents to KMOX where he was buried and forgotten. He left KMOX after less than a year, moved over to KWK, and was presently kicking the tar out of KSHE, his former station. After extensive surveys of the St. Louis radio audience, the KSHE brass had constructed a one-sentence mission statement: "To re-acquire the ex-KSHE listener." In short, the KSHE listeners were now turning their dials to KWK with Mark Klose. KSHE wanted them back.

KSHE's ratings, as a whole, had fallen dangerously low; their numbers for the morning show were at their lowest level in recent history.

On my third day in St. Louis, I was taken to lunch by the KSHE managerial team. (And where to my surprise, I learned that the station's program director was a graduate of my high school's archenemy, Brother Rice High School. I wisely decided I wouldn't let *that* get in the way.) After some pleasantries, I was asked "The Question." I gave an honest answer. I told them I felt there was either something indigenous to this community that would cause listeners to reject what I do ... or that I'd own the city in less than a year.

An amused general manager, John Beck, asked if I could do it for $35,000 a year. I responded that I could do it a lot better for $40,000. We agreed on $38,000. I was given a company car so that I could begin looking for an apartment. A week later I was back in Buffalo, and all my earthly belongings were carefully loaded into a moving van headed for St. Louis.

I got into town late one Sunday afternoon in May and, again, checked into the Airport Marriott. A young guy working the desk noticed my bill had been prepaid by KSHE. He proudly announced he was attending broadcasting school in the evening, and asked what I was going to be doing for KSHE.

"I'm going to take this town over," I cockily responded. He forced a smile, and handed over my room key.

"It's a game that can't be won. Only played."
—Will Smith from *The Legend of Bagger Vance*

Chapter 7

The word "luxurious" was not a word one used to describe KSHE studios in Crestwood, Missouri. From the outside the building resembled some sort of equipment shed. The inside could have been described as "early trailer court," complete with archaic, brown paneling and with a thin layer of crud covering almost everything. The tiny, on-air studio measured ten by twelve feet with once-white, acoustic ceiling tiles discolored from years of cigarette smoke. The final touch was "the KSHE window."

On my first tour through the building I was startled to see a large group of high school kids standing at the window to the studio, just staring in at the guy on the air from only a few feet away. I was told about the "tradition" the window signified, and about the many dubious "transactions" that had occurred there over the years.

The studio equipment looked like something out of the Marconi era, and the conditions were so cramped that having more than two people inside at a time would have seemed completely impractical.

John Ulett, a veteran of the station for ten years, was going to be my newsman and partner. John quickly realized that things were going to be different around the station. I told him that although we'd have to look at each other across two rooms and four panes of discolored glass, I'd be turning his microphone on every time I turned on my own. I also stressed that regardless of any restrictions he had once had on the morning show, he would now have the opportunity to spread his wings as my partner. John's reaction was simultaneously, if possible, one of eagerness and of reticence.

I wrote up a long list of necessities for the engineering department, such as some sort of mechanism to tape and play back phone calls. Then I headed back to the hotel to prepare for the first show. "Morning Sickness," as the show would be known, with J.C. and John was about to hit the air.

Since the system was not yet set up to put phone calls on the air, I spent the first few days at KSHE just sort of fooling around and trying to let everyone know that everything was about to change. I began with David Bowie's "Suffragette City," whose fans know that there's a pause in the middle of the song before he sings, "Wham, bam, thank you, ma'am!" When I played it, however, I hit the stop button at the moment of that pause, producing dead air for about fifteen or twenty seconds. Then I'd pop my microphone on and say, "Dave? Dave? DAVID!!," at which point I would hit the start button again. It may not seem like much now, but I assure you this sort of thing was considered a big deal in the summer of 1984. Nobody had ever done **anything** like that before on St. Louis FM radio. I also peppered the show with sound bites from old TV shows like *Leave It to Beaver*, and movies like *Airplane*. On "Twofer Tuesday," you'd often hear Kevin Bacon repeating the line from the fraternity scene in *Animal House*, "Thank you, Sir. May I have another?" "Meltdown Mitch," a burnout character from my time in Buffalo, popped up periodically with complaints about the rising prices demanded by ticket scalpers.

The audience noticed the changes almost immediately. And many of the listeners didn't like them one bit. The music purists thought I was messing with the "sanctity" of the music, and disliked the way in which it was being presented.

Gradually, however, the listeners began to "get" what I was doing. And even though I hated doing the extra day, it was the more relaxed atmosphere of the Saturday morning show that really created my bond with the listeners. The entire pace was different. I was in the studio alone—no news or traffic reports and fewer commercials than weekday programming. It was just me, two turntables, a microphone and a phone.

Just a few weeks into that summer of 1984, my parents decided to come down from Chicago for a weekend visit. I knew they would be listening to the Saturday morning show, so on the Friday morning before their arrival, I told our listeners I wanted them to call in the next morning and say, "J.C., you're such a nice boy. You must have wonderful parents!" I really didn't think anyone would even remember, but as my mom and dad listened to the show, almost every single person who called in that morning delivered that line. The playful exchange went on for the entire four hours, and the audience loved the chance to be in on the joke.

We would frequently air the recorded voice of the Centerre Bank's "time and temperature lady." One morning when the automated system was down, listeners quickly began calling in with wild theories about where she might be and why she might be out sick.

The high school kids were really gravitating to the show. I continued a feature I'd started in Buffalo called "High School Hotline," where kids could call in and report things like toe-jam outbreaks at their pool or cafeteria workers with open sores. After meeting the homecoming queen of a local high school where I was a guest speaker, on the air the next morning I offered to drink her bath water if she'd go out with me.

I'd started going to as many Cardinal games as I could and quickly realized KMOX's high-profile presence at the stadium was a nut I had to crack. Ulett alerted me as to how vigilant KMOX was about their broadcast rights of baseball, but after a KMOX banner contest at the ballpark that had come off completely lame, I decided it was time for the first "KSHE Completely Unauthorized Banner Contest." This idea presented a major problem for the Cardinals, who were stuck in the middle of a banner battle between KMOX and its fearless leader Bob Hyland, and KSHE and me. To further complicate matters, I demanded on the air that stadium organist, Ernie Hays play "Louie, Louie" while everyone held up their banners after the Cardinals batted in the fifth inning.

Close to a hundred banners splashed with my name and the KSHE logo sprouted up over the ballpark that night. And though the volume was reduced dramatically, the melody "The Kingsmen" had immortalized more than twenty years ago echoed throughout the stadium. Perhaps, more important, we demonstrated to the Cardinals, to KMOX and to ourselves that we had become something that would neither be intimidated nor go away.

It was about this time that Cardinals ace reliever, Bruce Sutter, announced he would be leaving the team. I theorized on air that if Bruce could just understand how strongly we felt about him, maybe he'd reconsider. Thus, we instituted "Nosehairs for Bruce," in which listeners would have to endure the incredibly painful process of pulling out a nosehair, tape it to a piece of paper, and mail it to us so we could deliver all the entries to Bruce at the stadium. Hundreds poured into the station over the course of the next few days, but the most memorable one came from a listener who wrote:

> "Dear J.C.
> I don't have any nosehairs, so I'm sending you the next best thing."

Taped to the paper was ... well ... I guess you can figure it out.

Another bit that garnered a great deal of attention was something I called the "One Hour Dirty Joke." Back in those days, you couldn't get away with telling the kinds of dirty jokes you can today. But I asked myself, What if we had an entire hour separating the set-up from the punchline? Then listeners who claimed to be offended would have to have to go out of their way to call in, right? So every morning at 7:15 while a song was playing, I'd record the jokes that listeners phoned in. Then I'd play back the first half of the joke, stopping the tape a split-second before the punchline. Then at 8:15, I'd play the punchline.

Not only was the feature a huge hit, but it also forced listeners to come back to the station an hour later, which proved extremely beneficial to our ratings.

I really enjoyed my on-phone time with the listeners. Subjects ranged from personal relationships to politics, from the serious to the downright silly. For totally cheap laughs, we once pumped about three balloons full of helium into St. Louis native and July 1983 *Playboy* centerfold Ruth Guerri.

And, of course, there was "Partytown."

For years I had wanted to initiate some sort of official kick-off to the weekend on Friday mornings. So I took an obscure Glenn Frey song from the *No Fun Aloud* album, and invited everyone from the *entire* KSHE staff to join me in the studio. After each KSHE employee had been identified and accounted for, I proceeded to crank the song as loud as it would go while turning on the mic for the live inserting of the song's "Yeah! Yeah!" reprise.

You just never know in this business. This once-obscure song was to become my trademark for the next twelve years.

The sales department at the station was beginning to see dollar signs, and they soon booked me for appearances at every bar, stereo shop, health club, and car dealer in the area. The crowds were huge, with long lines wrapped around the buildings outside. Some of the club appearances got so wild that people were grabbing at my clothes. The station's softball games, which usually had a handful of spectators, now had crowds of two hundred and more. A trip to a Cardinals game meant requests for autographs and free beer from fans. I found the attention remarkable, as well as somewhat mysterious, since I was, after all, only on radio.

Well, I did get on TV a few times. I had read in the paper that the head of "Fredbird," the Cardinal mascot, had been stolen, and we offered a reward for its safe return. And wouldn't you know? That "Fredbird" head showed up at the front door of the station the next morning. My television appearance came about when I presented it to the Cardinals at a news conference the next day. I also made the news when KMOV's Jim Bolen included me in one of those obligatory ratings sweeps in a multi-part series about morning radio, dubbing me "the bearded elf of dawn." (I actually dug that description.) And one by one, every television station, newspaper, magazine, cable show, high school and college publication asked me for an interview. (I think I did every single one.) The station manager even scheduled a lunch for me to meet a writer for the *St Louis Post-Dispatch*. He turned out to be a fellow by the name of Eric Mink, a quirky, cynical, sarcastic but very bright and amusing guy.

Agencies, public relations firms, concert promoters and TV stations began begging us for airtime to promote their events. We reciprocated these appeals by turning those requests into exclusive appearances by national celebrities connected to those events. For example, if the *Sally Jessy Raphael* show (which was taped at the KSDK television studios in St. Louis until the late 1980s) had *Wheel of Fortune* host, Pat Sajak, in town for a taping, we would arrange for Pat to be in the studio with us that morning. This arrangement made Sally's people happy, KSDK happy, and, naturally, KSHE staffers happy, too.

Pat Sajak was great (if not exactly happy with callers' suggestions about Vanna), and comedian Tim Conway was so funny he had us in tears. Bob Eubanks, host of the *Newlywed Game*, regaled us with stories about promoting Beatles' concerts back in L.A., long before his days of hosting game shows.

It seemed as if everybody in St. Louis was listening to us. Even our competitors appeared dumbfounded and unable to counter-program.

Things couldn't have been going any better. It felt great to be back in the Midwest, I was dating someone I really liked, and my parents were happy for me for the first time in a long time. What could go wrong?

I should have known better.

> *"Results? Why, man, I have gotten a lot of results. I know several thousand things that won't work."*
>
> **—Inventor Thomas Edison**

Chapter 8

I t was late in the summer of 1984, and "Morning Sickness" had been on the air about three months. The *Riverfront Times* had just published its first, long-form cover story on me, and subsequent "Letters to the Editor" were coming back mixed, to say the least. One reader called me the heir apparent to the Jack Carney empire. Another accused me of attempting to portray myself as a "macho, John Wayne type." Silly as the hoopla all seemed, I thought it was great we were getting so much publicity.

John Ulett still wasn't comfortable with our partnership. On the one hand, he was nervous about all the controversy we were constantly stirring up. On the other hand, Ulett did enjoy Cardinals' Tom Herr and other players addressing him as the "U Man," a nickname I had given him. This familiarity meant even the KMOX Cards were listening to our show.

KSHE's general manager, John Beck, and program director, Rick Balis, asked me to meet them for lunch one day at a conference center on Watson Road. When I arrived, I was shown to a meeting room where I found both men seated at an enormous table designed to accommodate a large group. At the center of the table was a tape recorder.

I didn't like the looks of this.

John said he had something to play for me, and pressed the start button on the recorder. The audition tape I had sent the station six months earlier to get the job began filling the room. After it was over, Beck and Balis complained that what I was now doing each day on the air at KSHE differed greatly from the style that was on the tape.

I explained that in Buffalo I had used a lot more character voices, plus prepared and pre-recorded bits, and that this former style of mine was already out of vogue. I also argued that I was going with my instinct toward more phone calls, interviews and spontaneous conversation. To their credit Beck and Balis listened, even though I sensed a lot of skepticism. They both insisted I replace the moniker "Morning Sickness" with the entirely innocuous, "Morning Zoo."

I left the meeting feeling I was on the ropes.

For the next few weeks, I felt as though every bit I did on the air was being put under a microscope. The station's consultant felt the show was out of control, and insisted I drop any features overtly appealing to the high school crowd. He presented me with a list of "recommended" bits; routines he had collected from radio stations across the country, which he had heard in the process of "fixing" their stations. Essentially, I was being asked to steal other people's material. Trying to hold the situation at bay, I began throwing in the kinds of bits Howard Stern in New York and Steve Dahl in Chicago had made famous, like "Blues News." It wasn't long before "Letters to the Editor" in the *Riverfront Times* pointed out that these routines were stolen from other morning shows. That was the end of *that* idea.

Around this time, rumors began surfacing that KSHE's new owners were engineering a deal to swap stations with the owners of the legendary WLUP in Chicago. This action would mean new owners, lots of instability and job losses. I also began getting calls from the program director at KMOX, Bob Osborne, who had heard about a big opening at a station in Houston; a job he believed I would be perfect for.

Then in early September of 1984, the president of Emmis Broadcasting and the group program director who oversaw all their stations arrived in St. Louis. I met with them in what had to be one of the *strangest* meetings I have ever been a part of.

KSHE's style of music is, of course, legendary. In the old days, the term "rock station" was synonymous with KSHE. But mainstream music was beginning to creep onto the playlist at an uncomfortable rate. The Scorpions, Judas Priest and AC/DC tunes were starting to give way to the lighter music of Huey Lewis and The News, Phil Collins and Billy Joel. I've never been a musical snob, but when our program director handed me the new Tina Turner single one morning while I was on the air, I was stumped as to how I was supposed to sell it to the audience. A few weeks later, I refused to play "Walkin' on Sunshine" by Katrina and The Waves again. (I received so many complaints from callers the first time I played it, that the entire show was forced to shut down for the better part of an hour.) I wasn't going to keep trying to con the audience into accepting this stuff.

But back to the meeting, which took place in General Manager John Beck's office in the prefab sales and management building adjacent to the KSHE studios. The agenda was made abundantly clear. The programming geniuses in Indianapolis had decided KSHE should move to a more mainstream sound, and new songs by Prince and Madonna were about to be added to the playlist. And they were counting on me to sell it to the KSHE audience.

For the next ninety minutes, all you could hear was the sounds of four grown men *screaming* at one another.

The company president and his programming "expert" insisted these songs would broaden the station's appeal. I, in turn, insisted the two admit themselves to a state hospital. After more than an hour of this, I offered to make a deal. I told them I'd do what they wanted if they gave me a company car. Completely baffled, they asked. "Why?" I answered, "If I play Prince and Madonna on KSHE, listeners are going to turn my car over in the parking lot. I want it to be yours, not mine."

They were not amused.

The meeting seemed to end in a draw. After I got home, I called the station in Houston, which had the opening I had heard about from Bob Osborne at KMOX. I figured I was going to need a job.

When I got off the air the next day, I was told KSHE's musical course would remain the same; there would be no changes. To this day, I wonder if anything I said at the meeting had persuaded them to change their minds. The station never brought the subject up again, and we went about our business on the morning show.

But things were getting hectic around the station. Pat Crocker, one of our account executives, had been working on the station's sponsorship of a series of comedy shows at the Westport Playhouse, where I would be the emcee. The first one in September of 1984 featured Larry "Bud" Melman from *Late Night with David Letterman*, Paula Poundstone, Wil Shriner and an up-and-coming comedian, Jerry Seinfeld. After the first two shows sold out, the promoter quickly locked us in for several more, including Jay Leno, Steven Wright, Sam

Kinison, Howie Mandel, Steve Landesburg, David Brenner, Roseanne, and Robert Klein, to name just a few. The performers would call in to the morning show to promote ticket sales, which helped our ratings. Better still, I got to hang out with the performers backstage while I emceed the show.

At one of the Playhouse shows, I thought I recognized a guy who was schmoozing with the promoters. It turned out to be KMOX legend Jack Carney.

Now, all I knew about Carney was that he was supposedly the biggest thing in radio in St. Louis. I also knew that he had taken a shot at me in the *Riverfront Times'* feature on me earlier that summer. When asked to comment on my sudden popularity, Carney had been quoted as saying, "That guy has to drop his pants to be able to count to eleven!" My response on the air was, "Well, Jack, at least I'd **get** to eleven instead of ten and a half like you would!"

The feud was on.

On the following Monday morning show, I took the opportunity to stick him. I remarked that KMOX must have been using his high school graduation picture for publicity, because when I saw him the other night, I thought he looked "like he had one foot in the grave." A few more smartass comments, and soon the entire radio community was abuzz with word that Carney was livid, demanding tapes of my show and threatening legal action. But nothing I'd said or done was, as they say in the legal profession, "actionable." I just sort of laughed the whole thing off.

Three days later, on a Thursday night, I got a call at my apartment telling me that Jack Carney had suffered a fatal heart attack while taking a scuba diving lesson at an indoor pool.

The next morning I delivered a brief, but respectful eulogy on the air. When I finished, the first call was from an extremely articulate, intelligent, credible-sounding guy who asked, "J.C.? Do you feel you can see death?"

Postscript: *The St. Louis newspapers crucified me about my 'one foot in the grave' remark.*

"When I was eighteen a Major League scout came to our house. He told my father, 'We want to sign your boy to a contract for five hundred dollars.' My dad said, 'This family just doesn't have that kind of money.'"

—Broadcaster/Actor Bob Uecker

Chapter 9

A few days after Carney's death, I picked up some sort of bug and ended up with a supreme case of laryngitis, which caused me to be off the air for a few days. The *Globe-Democrat*, in a clear case of wishful thinking, reported that "speculation was running rampant that I had been fired."

I got my voice back in time to fulfill a request I'd received to speak at a pep rally at St. Louis University High School on the eve of their big yearly match-up against rival, Vianney. Ever since I had found out that Mark Klose (my "radio rival") was a Vianney alum, I had been using the school's name as a punchline on the air. Presumably, that's why SLUH had invited me.

A prolonged, thunderous roar shook the place as I was introduced, and I vividly recall the concerned looks on the faces of the SLUH administrators. At that moment, my mind flashed back to my high school days, and I felt a tremendous sense of relief that I no longer had to answer to its authority. I confidently stepped to the podium.

"You may think you're going to walk away with this one, but I know for a fact that those Vianney guys think they're going to win this one!"

The cheers turned to boos.

"As a matter of fact, a carload of Vianney guys pulled up next to me on the way over here today and I could see they were totally pumped."

More boos.

"Now maybe you're saying to yourself, wait a minute. If they were only in a car next to you, how could you tell they were from Vianney? That's easy," I said. "When they reached up to pick their noses, I could see their class rings!"

Have you ever been at an air show and heard the deafening roar that rattles your teeth when the Blue Angels soar overhead? Imagine that sound times ten.

I had met Mark Klose earlier in the year. He had introduced himself to me, and I came away thinking he was the nicest guy in the world. Although we were in head-to-head competition and my entire professional existence hinged on beating him, knowing he was a good guy made it much more difficult for me to jerk him around on the air. My emotions were therefore mixed when I read in the paper a few days later that he had resigned from KWK.

The amount of time I had to put into the show heavily contributed to the end of the summer romance I'd been having with a beautiful girl from Illinois. But I had my eye on the consumer reporter from Channel Five, Anne Thompson, whom I frequently swooned over on the show. After grilling everyone in St. Louis media as to her availability, I announced that I planned to ask her out, live, on the air, during the annual "Old Newsboys Day" promotion directly in front of KSDK where we were scheduled to broadcast.

Anne was a beautiful blonde who had grown up on Cape Cod and attended Notre Dame. In other words, completely out of my league.

To my utter surprise, Anne seemed sort of tickled by the whole idea. And in front of a crowd of co-workers and fans, she agreed to go with me to the upcoming Bruce Springsteen concert.

When we walked into The Arena together a few nights later, we received a standing ovation from each section we passed on our way to our seats.

Pretty good first date, eh?

The next big concert to come through St. Louis was St. Louis favorite, Sammy Hagar. The station had arranged for me to introduce him onstage that night, so I arrived backstage early to record an interview with him. I asked him if there was anything special he wanted in the introduction, and he told me to just get the place revved up.

After welcoming the crowd and getting a plug in for the station, I asked the crowd of nearly twenty thousand for complete silence. Then I said, "Sammy's backstage right now wondering if you guys are excited about the show. So at the count of three, I want you to scream at the top of your lungs, 'HI, SAMMY!!!'"

Following the countdown, a roar that shook the paint chips from the rafters of the "Old Barn" must have rumbled its way into Sammy's dressing room. As I ran off the stage he met me halfway and, with eyes as big as saucers, he asked, "My God! What did you do out there?"

About that time, the first wave of new ratings for the summer of 1984 came in. We were exploding off the pages. The station immediately increased the cost of commercials on our show. Though a number of advertisers and ad agencies jumped ship claiming our show was offensive, the smart ones stayed on and many of KSHE's sales-people experienced a windfall. My $38,000 a year was nice, but...

I thought it was time to ask the station about a contract.

"Never fight an inanimate object."
—Author P.J. O'Rourke

Chapter 10

One of the last things "The Smash" had mentioned to me before I left DC 101 in Washington was that he had a family friend who practiced law in St. Louis. So when a radio pal suggested I look into incorporating, I called "Smash" for the guy's name.

I liked Jeff Gershman immediately. Not only did he quickly capture the essence of the situation, but I got a kick out of the fact that he seemed like a little kid trapped in a big, important lawyer's body. Jeff was an experienced tax attorney, and since I had never had any money to tax before, his help was invaluable. Within a few weeks Jeff had the papers drawn up, officially making me a "corporation." It was a move that ultimately proved highly beneficial, allowing substantial savings on my earnings in the years ahead.

Only much later did I discover that Jeff came from one of St. Louis' most prominent families and that his father owned half of the city of Clayton. This knowledge made me appreciate him even more. Here's a guy who could walk around with his chest out and his nose in the air, but instead, chose to treat a total idiot like me with complete respect. So when I decided to persuade KSHE into offering me a contract, I knew I wanted Jeff to negotiate the deal.

There are many disadvantages to working without a contract, especially when it comes to job security and money. So while management loved the ratings and revenue that came about as a result of my iconoclastic style, they could also pull the plug at any time without having to pay me a dime. In short, I was taking all the risks, and they were essentially risking nothing. Also, as the ratings swelled exponentially and the station reaped the financial benefits, I continued to make the same amount of money, with no increases and no bonuses. And no written contract.

I now felt my future was in St. Louis, and I wanted some of the action. I wanted my first house. You might say I thought it was time for J.C. and KSHE to "get married."

Now, I liked the KSHE management guys. I had gotten over the fact that Program Director Rick Balis had gone to a high school I was bred to loathe. General Manager John Beck always had been upfront with me and I enjoyed making him laugh. Unfortunately, KSHE's idea of a contract was a simple two- or three-page work agreement; my lawyer and I wanted a more comprehensive document, which covered areas like severance, indemnification, ownership of creative ideas and characters, and so forth. (It's amazing the numerous icky things that have a way of causing problems down the road if they're not legally addressed in contractual form)

The process started to bog down over the next few weeks, and things became tense. Every time we'd put something in a draft, Emmis Broadcasting, the Indianapolis-based company who owned KSHE, would put something new in to counter it. The document was getting longer and longer. To his credit, John Beck took me to lunch in an effort to try to return things to a simpler form, but the whole thing had taken on a life of its own. Then, the unthinkable happened. Emmis' attorney indicated they might have to remove me from the air if no significant progress could be made soon. Christmas was only a few weeks away.

To further complicate matters, the KSHE marketing department had scheduled the production of an expensive television commercial designed to feature me. This meant that, in addition to the production costs, the actual time had to be purchased from the individual television stations weeks in advance. Though the actors had been hired and the studio time booked, if there wasn't going to be a "J.C. and The Morning Zoo," all of it had to be canceled. The clock was ticking.

One afternoon, after Jeff had spent most of the day trying to reach a resolution, he called to tell me the station's management was pulling me off the air.

Nervous about the tapes and materials I used on the show (and which had taken years to accumulate), I drove over to the studios in

Crestwood late that night to retrieve them. The locks had been changed.

The consultant who had initially hooked me up with the station called from L.A., screaming, "DO YOU KNOW HOW OUT OF LINE YOU ARE?"

Almost anti-climatically, we struck a deal a few days later; however, the contract was only for one year. Regardless, John Beck secretly arranged to have the **entire** staff greet me at 5:30 a.m. when I arrived for my first day back at work. That's the kind of guy he was.

The radio station Christmas party was scheduled for later that week at an area banquet hall. But the memo indicated the party would have a "fifties" theme. Now, I totally understood that the owners of Emmis Broadcasting were Jewish, and that the word "Emmis" (as in Emmis Broadcasting) is Hebrew for "truth." But if you're going to say it's a Christmas party, shouldn't the theme be … well … Christmas?

The president of the company gave out 13-inch color televisions to each member of the full-time air staff. True to form (and because I absolutely loathe the idea of dressing up in a costume for *any* reason), I came to the party in a windbreaker. When asked why I hadn't dressed in the "fifties" style, I replied, "This is what I wear when it's in the fifties."

But as I took my seat, I told myself, "Shut up, J.C. You just got a free color TV."

"Nothing good ever happens after midnight."
—"Grandpa" Ulett

Chapter 11

The ratings for the fall of 1984 came out in January of 1985. We were growing at an unprecedented rate. The station was erupting into such a powerhouse that our competitors evidently decided playing dirty would be the only way to stop us.

Examples?

A few days before his St. Louis concert date, John Ulett had made some unflattering remarks on the air about the condition of rock star Bryan Adams' face which, as you may have noticed, isn't what you'd call "smooth." Some morons from KWK played the tape of John's comments for Adams backstage just before our interview with him. You can imagine the reception we got from Adams and his people.

Y98 had begun recording and excerpting the roughest examples of language on the show, then editing long strings of these out-of-context remarks together and sending the tapes to advertisers and agencies, hoping they would cancel their commercials.

The owner of a low-rated, soft-rock station went beserk when I wondered on the air if "its broadcast tower fell in the middle of an empty forest, would anybody hear the station?" The owner actually called me, then my lawyer, indicating that "things would start happening" to me but that I wouldn't know "who was behind these things." Now, I may not be the brightest bulb in the box, but that sounded like a threat, so we cease-and-desisted him. He responded by blowing up the letter to poster size, and hanging it in the lobby of his station. I guess he showed us, eh?

In addition, our sources at KMOX indicated the station was regularly sending tapes of our show to the FCC, hoping to get us in trouble with the feds.

The high (or should I say the low?) point of this "let's-get-'em" insanity came when I heard from an extremely reliable source at the *Post-Dispatch* that Bob Hyland was looking for dirt on me. Hyland had told the reporter that he had corralled his pals in the Florissant police department (as well as the Major Case Squad!) to try to dig up anything that might be potentially damaging to my reputation. Hyland's specific instructions, I was informed, included looking in the area of "scandals, unpaid bills and bastard children." (Don't think for a minute that I didn't start driving home at night staring into the rear-view, or jumping up in the middle of the night after hearing a noise.)

Of course the beauty of Hyland's scheme for me, was that I knew no one was going to find anything. I hadn't been an angel my whole life, but I didn't have any huge skeletons in the closet, either. Still, powerful people in this city, some viewed as pillars of the community, had left me feeling incredibly violated.

Everyone at the station was getting tired of being pushed around, and collectively decided to fight back. When the manager of the band "Nightranger" got huffy with KSHE's programming department and went over to KWK exclusively, I was essentially told to retaliate by trashing the band. With some modifications on Jay Leno's very old stand-up act (where he attacked carnival workers as a "syphilitic tribe of gypsies with no birth records of any kind"), I reeled off a version of that riff against the band on the air a few mornings later. Actually, it was pretty funny, and I'm fairly certain most listeners got the idea we were just jerking back at some guys who had jerked us around first.

About a week later, I received word Jack Blades, one of the members of "Nightranger," intended to file a multi-million dollar lawsuit. I hadn't known it at the time, but it turned out Blades was from St. Louis, still had family here, and was claiming in the suit that I'd said he had syphilis.

The national trade magazines really ran with this one. But after a few weeks of lawyers on both sides huffing and puffing and threatening to blow each other's houses down (not to mention Emmis threatening to pull every single song from the band's record label from all of its stations, nationwide) cooler heads prevailed, and the suit never materialized.

It was definitely time for a diversion, and we came up with a terrific idea called, "Jamaica Tape for the Morning Zoo?" For the chance at winning one of five trips for two to Ocho Rios, Jamaica, listeners were asked to make a tape, ninety seconds in length, with an original song extolling the virtues of KSHE, our show, and Budweiser, the trip's sponsor.

Aside from a sunburn that brought me within hours of being admitted to the hospital (or the "Human Repair Center" as it's called in that part of the world), the trip and accompanying live broadcasts were a rousing success. It also represented the first-ever week of international broadcasts by a St. Louis radio station.

Once back home, we learned the consultants had been in town and had recommended we add a woman to the morning show. They felt the show sounded too much like a locker room, and a woman's presence might work to counter-balance that perception.

Nancy Crocker was the wife of one of my favorite KSHE account executives, Pat Crocker. Nancy had dabbled in free-lance commercial voice-over and corporate training film work, and she fit the job description at the time: "cheap" and "available."

The experiment proved disastrous. The initial research showed that our audience actually preferred the sophomoric style John and I had perfected, and Nancy was perceived as having ruined that chemistry. In addition, tension developed between John and Nancy, and there were several angry exchanges between them. I could tell John was concerned that Nancy was trying to horn in on his territory, and while I thought Nancy was a riot, I could also see John's point. Management finally stepped in, and the experiment was discontinued after only a few short months.

It wasn't long before the buzz in local media circles was that I was the one Nancy couldn't get along with, and the one who had forced her out. But while that misconception annoyed me, I had my hands full trying to deflect attacks from every other conceivable direction. Women's groups said I was hostile to women. Gay groups said I was hostile to gays. The gearheads and hoosiers said I was too upscale and the yuppies said I was just another stereotypical FM jock wearing a black T-shirt.

At least that's what people *said*. What they *did* was apparently another story, since our ratings continued to soar. Even *Post-Dispatch* columnist, Jerry Berger, who had written more than one unflattering piece about me, was now recognizing the impact I had made on the community.

My newfound "celebrity" was now affording me opportunities I wouldn't have had otherwise. The station hired a helicopter and pilot to pick me up at Spirit of St. Louis Airport and fly me into Six Flags' "Senior Night," where I introduced "Blue Oyster Cult" to the waiting throng. Cool.

But being a "celebrity" didn't necessarily translate into acting or feeling like one, as the story of my interview with actress Helen Slater reveals. This young, beautiful blonde had starred in the movie, *Supergirl*, a few years earlier, and was currently on a twenty-one city tour to publicize her new film, *The Legend of Billie Jean*. During our interview, I could have *sworn* this gorgeous star was flirting with me, but self-consciously dismissed that as mere wishful thinking. But after the interview, she met briefly with her road manager, walked back over to me, and asked if I could join her for lunch.

What? Do I **look** stupid?

I met her at the Tenderloin Room in the Chase-Park Plaza shortly after one that afternoon. The flirting continued, but I was way too nervous to ask for her phone number in L.A. She gave me a gentle kiss goodbye, and that was the last time I saw her; at least, that is, until her appearance several weeks later on the *Tonight Show* with substitute host, Joan Rivers.

When Rivers asked what she'd been doing lately, Helen filled her in about the nationwide tour she'd been on. "Do they ask you the same questions over and over everyplace you've been?" Rivers asked. "No! Not at all," she replied. "I've been meeting a lot of really nice people, like in St. Louis. Really, really wonderful people."

Hmmm. I guess that's what I get for being chicken!

The following day, everyone wanted to talk about Helen and what she'd said on the show. Then, several weeks later, I opened a letter on the air. It contained a clipping from one of the supermarket rags, implying that Helen Slater was dating Michael J. Fox (she would go on to appear with him in the film, *The Secret of My Success*).

I acted as though I was heartbroken and distraught. My voice cracked. I tried to sound as though I was on the verge of weeping. I jokingly speculated that "maybe Hinckley had the right idea," and that I "might not be on the show the next day because I might have to go to Washington." Of course, anyone with any brains knew I was goofing on the John Hinckley-obsession-with-Jodie Foster-and-subsequent-attempted-assassination-of-President Reagan scenario. But, when I got off the air, the station managers pulled me into an office where two, very large Secret Service agents were waiting for me. They informed me that they'd received information that I had made a possible threat against the life of President Reagan, and that law demanded I be "detained" while they completed their investigation and evaluation.

Even I knew it was time to shut up.

After about ninety minutes, the two agents appeared satisfied I was not a threat to society (or the President). They seemed like decent guys, and I asked them who had called in about me. They told me it was against policy to reveal that information, but when I blurted out, "Was it KMOX?" their heads snapped in each other's direction. I was convinced that KMOX had been at the bottom of this farce.

The story ran as a headline the next day. As I read it, I remember thinking that I'd come to St. Louis to do a humorous radio show and now I was being depicted as a potential presidential assassin. And I was definitely starting to lose my sense of humor about Bob Hyland and his boys at KMOX.

It was well known in the local broadcasting business that Hyland loathed television, and theories abounded as to why. Some thought Hyland believed television hurt radio's ratings; others, that he was repeatedly irritated by the stream of KMOX/KHTR personalities who jumped mediums for more money and more prestige. I felt that it was simply another case of Hyland being a control freak.

Regardless, it came as quite a shock to many industry observers when it was announced Hyland had given the green light to a television show on Channel Four called "Hot Hit Video," which would be hosted by a different KHTR disc-jockey each week. But when the program debuted, it was immediately revealed that Hyland had approved the show with the proviso that the face of the talent never be shown on-camera. All the audience could see of the host was a lot of giant hats, odd lighting and distant camera angles and reverse shots. I railed about this on the air each week which, we heard, drove Hyland crazy.

KSHE caught a major break in the spring of 1985 when Channel Five's pre-game Cardinal baseball show, "Cardinal Control," came to the station one morning to tape a piece on John Ulett. Ostensibly it was to be a feature about John and his role as public address announcer at Busch Stadium, but when the story aired a few days later, it might as well have been a twelve-minute commercial for "J.C. and The Morning Zoo." God, was it funny.

Though we felt as though we were on a roll, not everything went according to plan.

I thought it would be funny to have the most-famous voice in television game shows, Johnny Olsen, record a series of drop-ins for the show. We contacted his people, the station cut a check, and I overnighted the scripts to him. Two nights later I was driving home from dinner in the Central West End when a news report said Johnny Olsen had passed away that evening. I always wondered if it was because of something he read in those scripts.

But the battle lines had been clearly drawn, and war between Hyland's KMOX and our station broke out during the 1985 Veiled Prophet Fair, which was held over the Fourth of July on the Arch grounds.

KSHE General Manager John Beck's plan was to take the station right down Main Street. He had approached VP officials about allowing us to broadcast from a booth on the Arch grounds during the event, but he was turned down.

All I really knew about the VP Fair was what I had been told, but with its masks, mystery identities and rituals, the event sounded a lot like the KKK to me. I had also heard that the big joke around town was the fair officials' over-inflated crowd estimates and unsubstantiated boast that it was "America's biggest birthday party." And, furthermore, that the VP "queen" was always the daughter of some rich guy, and was usually ugly.

You can imagine, then, how I bowed to the radio gods upon hearing this year's "Queen of Beauty and Love" was the daughter of none other than KMOX's leader Bob Hyland. After all, here was a guy who had engaged in every underhanded trick to try to run me out of town. So, even though it may have seemed mean to some, I joked that "this was the first year that the VP Fair queen was so ugly they decided to put the mask over *her* face."

Undaunted by the snub from Fair officials, John Beck secured rights to the *Admiral* riverboat on the Mississippi River. It was a stroke of genius! Though the river was directly adjacent to the Arch grounds, it wasn't actually *part of* the sacred territory. So here we were, pumping out a zillion watts of sound onto the eastern edge of the fairgrounds, and there wasn't a thing fair officials could do to stop us. Except, of course, stand by and fume.

The *Admiral,* a once-hopping entertainment and excursion vessel, was now nothing more than a bombed-out hulk of steel, complete with jagged beams and holes in the floor that went all the way down to the water. Once aboard, we simply set up a table and a set of enormous speaker columns, and went on the air. Each day, crowds gathered along the shore of the river to watch us do the show; in the afternoon, the number of spectators reached four thousand-plus for our live "Partytown" show.

Bob Hyland had successfully convinced fair officials (and himself) that only KMOX should have any official presence during the three-day event so, of course, our set-up drove him insane. In retaliation, Hyland sent the station's helicopter to buzz over our crowd.

The next day, I mounted the wireless microphone unit on my back and strolled the two hundred feet down the river to the *President* riverboat, from which KMOX was broadcasting. The "Voice of St. Louis" had hired a guy named Arnie Warren to replace the late Jack Carney, and we'd been making him the butt end of a lot of jokes on the air. We knew that Arnie was doing his show from the vessel's third level, so John, D.J. and I each bought a ticket for five dollars. As we boarded the boat, we provided a play-by-play for the listeners at home, as well as for the growing crowd watching along the banks of the river.

Arnie's guests were *Adam 12* star, Kent McCord; *Playboy* centerfold, Marlene Jansen; and *Airplane* star, Robert Hays; all of whom were in town to promote a racetrack event being held across the river in Illinois. They had all been our guests on the *Admiral* the day before.

As soon as Robert Hays saw us, he literally fell off his chair. We didn't do anything specifically to disrupt the show, but our mere presence sent KMOX staffers into a tizzy. Not until a KMOX auxiliary staffer grabbed me and actually began to interfere with our broadcast did things start to get tense, and we left of our own volition. The crowd, now doubled in size, greeted us with a standing ovation as we exited the boat.

We finished off three days of live broadcasts from the 1985 VP Fair with one of the largest, most enthusiastic crowds I've ever appeared before. Several days later, Eric Mink wrote a hilarious story about our VP broadcasts for the *Post-Dispatch*. After all, we had pulled off a stunning coup. The officials had shunned us, and had made it clear they believed we didn't even merit space on the fair grounds. But the numbers clearly proved otherwise.

Postscript: *A giant, full-color VP brochure was issued seeking so-*

licitation for next year's event. A sizable portion of the piece was de-voted to "youth involvement." It featured a large photograph of ... you guessed it ... the huge crowd taking part in the final "Partytown," with fists in the air, screaming "Yeah! Yeah!" The photo matched up per-fectly with our own shots of the event. But the photo wasn't even taken on the fair grounds. VP organizers had treated us like dirt, yet they unashamedly used our success to promote the event.

"Your ambitions exceed your abilities."
—WMEE General Manager Bob Elliot

Chapter 12

I never thought I'd live to see the day.

An old college friend of mine who was working for Gundaker Realtors found me a modest, three-bedroom house in Ballwin and, more important, explained that I could actually afford it. At age thirty-one I was finally a homeowner. Sometimes, I would just walk out into the street and stare at the house. I couldn't believe that just two years ago I'd been living in a rat hole apartment in Buffalo.

I was even blessed with great neighbors in Ed and Ellen Alberding and their family. One afternoon the doorbell rang, and standing there was Doug Wickenheiser of the St. Louis Blues, who explained he lived down the street. As time went on, "Wick" would frequently come over to watch the fights I'd order on pay-per-view. That is, when he wasn't busy placing lawn jockeys he'd swiped from the neighborhood on **my** lawn. Domestically, life wasn't bad.

Professionally, I was so tired of people taking cheap shots at us that I guess I actually began looking for fights. One evening, *PM Magazine*, a sappy show which KTVI aired at 6:30, announced the show would be featuring "St. Louis' favorite morning shows" for the next two weeks. The next morning, I went on the air and made a big stink about the fact that we'd been excluded. I railed on the show and insisted everyone call Channel Two to complain. Apparently, a lot of people did, because Channel Two's general manager called complaining to my boss that they couldn't even conduct business because the switchboard was flooded. (If that was the case, I wondered how he got an outside line, but that's not important now. Less than a year later, *PM Magazine* would be canceled.)

In the summer of 1985, the St. Louis football Cardinals held a luncheon for all the local radio stations at a fancy eatery in the Central West End. As I walked in to the crowded room, I could hear Y98's Guy Phillips speaking in a voice clearly designed to be heard by all, saying, "Yeah. J.C. gets his name in the paper all the time 'cuz he b***s Jerry Berger!" Two of my fellow KSHE "boss jocks" quickly tackled me to prevent bloodshed.

But I'd soon have the last laugh.

I had continued to occasionally date Channel Five's Anne Thompson. One day, she told me that then-KSDK anchorman Dick Ford had suggested the station approach me about doing something for their news show that might bring in some new, younger viewers. Someone at Channel Five must have liked the idea, because Anne set up a meeting at Bristol's for an introduction to the station's special projects producer, Ava Ehrlich, a few days later. I'm absolutely certain Ava was expecting a real dirt bag, but we hit it off immediately. I was asked to cut an audition tape the following week, with the understanding that I would write, produce, and edit the piece myself.

I chose to do a story on "Open Mic Night" at the Funnybone Comedy Club at Westport. I set up the interviews, directed my photographer as to what I wanted shot, cut a standard "stand-up" in which I delivered part of the story while on-camera in front of the club, and called it a night. The next day, with editing help from the brilliant Ellen Gomez DeFillipo, I submitted the piece to Ava. A day later she called to tell me I had the job as Channel Five's new entertainment reporter and that the story on the Funnybone would air as my first piece. KSDK issued a fancy press release, and I was off to Beltone in South City to be fitted for my earpiece. Then I went to Crestwood Plaza to buy some new shirts. Hey! I was gonna be on TV.

The Funnybone story aired on the five o'clock news the following week. I was on the set with Dick Ford and Jennifer Blome to introduce and tag the piece. It went like a charm, and afterwards I met with Ava to discuss some ideas for upcoming stories.

Don't get me wrong. I expected some criticism. But the next morning when I picked up the *Globe-Democrat*, a story with the headline: "Corcoran Tamed for the Tube," appeared. (The *Globe-Democrat* had been writing not-so-nice stuff about me since I'd hit town, but I sort of ignored them since I'd never met anybody who claimed to have ever actually read it.) The story was written by longtime radio personality, "Johnny Rabbitt," who, under his real name, Ron Elz, was attempting a daily, Jerry Berger-style column. (I actually thought this was a good move for Elz since his radio act basically consisted of wearing a derby with two giant bunny ears protruding from the bill, and a delivery right out of the 1950s.)

Elz' September 27, 1985, column read in part:

"Corcoran tried to take his act to the tube. Hopefully, viewers practiced their own version of Corcoran's 'what you want' shtick after hearing him for ten seconds. That's about all they really got to see of Corcoran since KSDK wisely kept him off camera most of the time. Corcoran was on-camera only toward the close of the bit, sporting a tie, no less, and looking more than a little leery of the camera. A good lesson for all of us is that the cocky Corcoran of radio, who acts as if no one can tell him what to do, obviously has been told what not to do."

I could not believe a newspaper would just let a reporter make that much stuff up. Had Elz made so much as *one* call to the newsroom, he would have been informed that I had written and produced the entire piece myself and that the amount of on-camera time I had been given was my own choice.

This would be the first of several run-ins I was to have with the *Globe.*

About that time, the ratings for the spring of 1985 were released. I'd now been in St. Louis a full year, and the numbers showed we had passed everyone but KMOX across the board. Bonus money was rolling in. We were getting publicity everywhere. I was receiving anywhere from a hundred to three hundred fan letters a week. Then, one day the phone rang. It was the general manager of KLOS in Los Angeles.

Three days later I was sitting across from him and his program director at Lambert Airport. They told me they were very unhappy with their current morning show, and then offered me the job on the spot. But when we began talking salary, the offer was for just slightly less than what I was making at KSHE. After asking about this, the GM went into a little speech. He explained that almost all of their on-air talent had side deals or hosted game shows or pitched movie scripts, which brought in additional income. Then I sort of innocently asked, "Did you ever think that just might be the reason why you're not happy with the way your jocks sound?"

They got back on the plane to L.A., and I never heard from KLOS again.

The Iranians started acting up again that summer. But unlike the other morning shows and news outlets with their somber approach, John Ulett and I saw it as an opportunity to say what we knew many folks out there were thinking: We're fed up with the whole, goofy country! So one morning, we decided to call Iran.

The ridiculous studio set-up at KSHE actually worked to our advantage since John, who was in another studio two rooms over from me, could talk to the overseas operator without my voice feeding back down the line. When John finally reached the Iranian airport, I was able to pepper the airwaves with jokes and sound effects that our listeners could hear, but those at the other end, couldn't. The language barrier alone accounted for many of the laughs as we asked for everything from the phone number for Iranian Fried Chicken to the time of their country's self-flagellation hour. One person not amused by the bit was *Post-Dispatch* media critic Eric Mink, who wrote a scathing column under the headline, "KSHE Dabbles in Foreign Policy." But, even today, that bit remains a favorite with fans, and the one most people want to talk about when I run into them on the street.

The Cardinals were playing great baseball in the summer of 1985 and, as usual, we were looking for a way to tie into the excitement of a first-place team. A friend gave me a New York City phone book, and one morning, we began randomly calling numbers, looking for Mets fans to bother. (We fiercely hated the Mets in those days and, most important, they were in second place!) We ended up on the phone with two, corner-store clerks from Queens named Ricky and Ronnie Espinosa. Both had come to America from Ecuador only a few years before and spoke little English. But they were very funny as they tried to figure out what we meant when we told them they were "on the radio in St. Louis."

After a few weeks of these daily phone calls, the station's marketing person asked me what I thought about flying the two to St. Louis for the Cards-Mets series at Busch. Of course, we built the excitement up to the level of a papal visit; when Ricky and Ronnie walked off that plane at Lambert, over a hundred listeners, TV cameras and even a live band greeted them.

After taking in the ballgame that night and making several of the ten o'clock news shows, we had the boys up early the next morning. They had to make a live appearance before yet another crowd gathered in front of the station and, before long, the two were signing autographs!

Before it was all over, Rawlings had donated a pair of baseball gloves and, because the two boys had remarked they watched ballgames on a small, black-and-white set, the station kicked in a color TV. Ricky and Ronnie were nearly in tears. We had taken two ordinary guys, and had given them their fifteen minutes of fame.

The Cardinals played their way into the 1985 League Championship Series against the Los Angeles Dodgers, and I begged the station to send us to L.A. to cover it. I'd listened to Steve Dahl and Garry Meier's Cubs coverage in San Diego (on WLS in Chicago) the year before, and knew how good it would sound to the St. Louis fans. It took some convincing, but PD Rick Balis and GM John Beck (to their credit) gave it the OK, and we were gone.

We set up in the lobby of the team hotel in L.A. and, because of the time change and scheduling of games in the afternoon or evening, went on the air four hours before each game. This meant we were usually on during the afternoon, St. Louis time. It wasn't uncommon for Tom Herr or Ozzie Smith to sit down at our table and chat awhile before it was time to catch the team bus to the ballpark. And since we were in the show-biz capital of the world, it meant almost anyone might go by. In fact, St. Louis native Mark Price, who played "Skippy" on the hit NBC series, *Family Ties*, sat in with us one afternoon. While he attempted to discuss his acting career, Andy Van Slyke riddled him with questions like, "Do you have a driver's license?" and "Are you old enough to shave?"

And I tell the following story only because it has been lied about for so many years, and because it involves one of St. Louis' most-respected personalities.

Our broadcast table was only a few yards from the hotel's front desk. Just a few minutes before we were to hit the air, I saw Jack Buck checking out. I decided this might be a chance to introduce myself and, at the same time, diffuse some of the hostility I'd heard Jack felt toward me. As you may recall, Jack Buck and Bob Hyland were extremely close, and Buck was aware of the bad blood that existed between his boss and me. Earlier in the season Ulett had told me that Buck was quizzing him about me. In particular, John told me Buck had asked if I was "a big guy," and when John informed him I wasn't, John said Buck broke into a boxing stance. He then proceeded to describe how he'd be able to quickly take me out with a left jab followed by a right cross.

Now, believe it or not, most people actually end up liking me once they get to spend a few minutes with me. In this case, I figured I'd wander over, extend my hand, tell him I was a fan of his and a huge fan of the game and, hopefully, clear up any misgivings between us. But Jack refused to shake my hand. In fact, he made it abundantly clear what he thought about me. I tried to explain that he'd probably heard only one side of the story with regard to the highly publicized feud with Bob Hyland, and that I wasn't such a bad guy. But Jack wasn't listening. Now, there were quite a few people in the lobby watching this exchange. I quietly told him I intended to stand in front of him with my hand out until he shook it, and that the longer this scene went on, the more likely it would be that he, not I, would end up looking bad. I also told him that I didn't want that, either. Jack reluctantly shook my hand. I said, "Thank you," and we went our separate ways. It would be eight years until we would shake hands or speak again.

On our last day in L.A., we finished the show and headed to Chavez Ravine. We watched Jack Clark hit his amazing shot over the head of Pedro Guerrero into the left-field bleachers, earning the Cardinals a place in the World Series.

When I got back to St. Louis, I was handed a phone message from WLS in Chicago. I was being offered a chance to go home and work at the station I'd dreamed about working at since I was a kid.

"You never look as good as you think you do when you win, and you never look as bad as you think you do when you lose."

—posted on Yankee clubhouse bulletin board

Chapter 13

I t was a very busy week.

The 1985 World Series opened in Kansas City and, again, KSHE General Manager John Beck pulled one out of his hat by securing broadcast lines and a spot in the Cardinals hotel in Overland Park, Kansas. When the series shifted back to St. Louis for games three, four and five, Ulett and I were surprised to find a Kansas City rock station set up across the hall from us at our studios in Crestwood.

The "Max Floyd and Frankie" show was broadcasting live back to Kansas City. Max was a burned-out, former program director who'd brought me to Atlanta seven years prior for a job interview, but when I reminded him of it, I don't think he remembered me or, for that matter, that he'd ever even been in Atlanta. Frankie, however, was a babe.

John and I went on the air that morning singing the praises of the Redbirds, giving away tickets and pumping the audience for Game 3. Max and Frankie did the same for their side right across the hall. But about two hours into the show, I remembered that all the studios in the building were actually electronically connected. If I could just find the right buttons to push, I'd be able to eavesdrop on their show. Sure enough, I discovered the correct combination of buttons just as our pals from Kansas City were railing on about our team, our city, and even *our* show. I quickly stopped the Aerosmith record I was playing, popped my microphone on, and explained the situation to the KSHE audience. Then I put ***their*** studio on ***our*** air. Suddenly, the St. Louis audience was listening to the venom the Kansas City show was spewing out. Then, in an amazingly colossal blunder, Max mentioned their show would be over at nine o'clock.

When Max and Frankie, adorned in their Royals jackets, left our building shortly after 9 a.m., they were "greeted" by about two dozen locals who'd been listening to their anti-St. Louis diatribe. The group felt compelled to let Max and Frankie know just what they thought of the "Max and Frankie" show.

We all had a pretty good laugh about it as we planned the next day's show and, though the timing couldn't have been worse, I had to leave early for the TV station to prepare for an interview I'd scheduled weeks earlier with Mr. Whipple. That's right, the "don't-squeeze-the-Charmin'" guy was scheduled to be in town, and I had to grab my crew and head to Schnucks in North County to meet up with him.

The guy had a fantastic act! Dressed only in his famous supermarket smock, which camouflaged a wireless microphone, he would wheel a cart full of bathroom tissue down the aisle and wait for elderly women to recognize him. (Yes, he was wearing pants!) Then he'd autograph a package of t.p., give the ladies a kiss, and move on. Naturally we had a camera hidden behind a display at the end of the aisle, and were catching all of this on tape.

We hauled ass back to the station at Tenth and Market where I wrote, edited and ran the story while exchanging every toilet paper joke in the book with Stan Stovall and Deanne Lane on the Channel Five set.

From there it was over to the Marriott, where I was to meet with the operations manager of WLS. This meeting was nothing to sneeze at; it was the big league calling. At the end of the meeting, it was decided that I'd come to Chicago in a few weeks for another visit.

To this day I couldn't tell you a thing that happened in Game 3, even though I was there.

Of course, the Cardinals lost the series in seven games, preceded by the now-infamous Don Denkinger flub at first base the night before. When we arrived at the Kansas City airport Monday morning, I ran into an old college friend who was working as an assistant to then-baseball commissioner, Peter Ueberroth. I asked the "commish" what he thought of Denkinger's call and he just rolled his eyes back in his head, suggesting that, just maybe, he'd heard enough about it.

Randy Raley was KSHE's afternoon disc jockey at the time. He'd come to St. Louis from Kansas City, and he made no effort to conceal the fact he was an avid Royals fan. However, most of us thought he'd pushed his luck entirely too far when he walked into work that afternoon sporting a Royals satin jacket. After all, we hadn't just lost a World Series, we'd had a national championship stolen. Raley may have been one of our own, but he still needed to be taught a lesson.

Randy was known for putting long records on the air, and then going to the parking lot for a smoke. I noticed he'd leave the jacket hanging on the back of his chair in the studio when he left, so I figured this was a good time for someone to slip in, grab the jacket and split. But evidently several of the guys in the building had something ... well ... more "dramatic" in mind. When I saw our promotions assistant leaving with a bucket, I knew the jacket wouldn't be hanging pretty for very long.

A small caravan of cars proceeded to Lone Elk State Park in the far western part of the St. Louis area. There the guys shoveled up a sizable quantity of bison excrement, and returned to the station parking lot. When Raley came out to his car at seven o'clock on that chilly October night, he found his car adorned with "souvenirs" from the park.

None of us ever saw the Royals jacket again.

(Ironically, several weeks later, Randy Raley gave out umpire Don Denkinger's home phone number on the air. The story made national news when Denkinger complained about receiving hundreds of calls. My mother called to tell me that "WGN radio in Chicago is jumping all over you!" It turned out the *AP*, without checking its facts, had attributed this stunt to me.)

In one of the most difficult decisions of my life, I passed on the offer to move back to Chicago and work for WLS. As I sat in the operation manager's office overlooking Lake Michigan, I had to be honest with myself. I was having more fun, getting more opportunity to do a variety of things I liked to do, and making more money in St. Louis than I would in Chicago.

The end of the year signaled the end of the fragile, one-year contract I'd signed the year before. It was also a repeat of the sabre-rattling we'd witnessed before when contract negotiations had initially failed, and I was once again subjected to being yanked off the air, having the locks changed on the building, and threatened with worse. Another one-year deal was finally agreed upon, but the outcome further damaged my already-tenuous relationship with Emmis Broadcasting headquarters in Indianapolis.

A recurring segment on the show was live coverage of the periodic launches of the space shuttle. Someone had given me a private number at NASA that allowed us to hear, and subsequently broadcast, all the conversations that went on between mission control and the shuttle crew. I liked to speak into my bullhorn during the lulls and provide phony dialogue about things like the shuttle bathroom and astronauts asking one another to scratch itches they couldn't reach. "Ooh ... Right ... oh ... No ... a little to the left ... yeah!"

I often remarked that the reason I aired those actual conversations was due to the fact that NASA would never tell us the truth about what happened if something should go severely wrong, or if the shuttle should ever blow up.

In January of 1986, the space shuttle *Challenger* did just that. The tragedy was compounded by the fact that the shuttle had on board its first private civilian—schoolteacher, wife and mother—Christa McAuliffe.

As is always the case when a tragedy occurs, the horror and sadness is quickly followed by a wave of macabre jokes. But this particular tragedy was so horrific and touched so many Americans on such an emotional level, that I made the decision not to allow shuttle jokes on the air. But because I'd done so much "shuttle humor" in the past and, presumably, because they just figured it "sounded like something he'd do," reports began circulating that we had been doing shuttle jokes on our show, after the disaster.

It was yet another example of the mainstream press printing an unsubstantiated story about me.

The ratings for the all-important, autumn 1985 period came out a few weeks later. It was an all-time high for the station and for "J.C. and The Morning Zoo." We were approaching KMOX territory, and our closest FM competitor had disappeared into the very distant horizon. Our numbers were now at a level more than thirty percent higher than any other FM morning show in St. Louis radio history. With our show spearheading the attack, KSHE had emerged from a second-class, "hippie" and "gearhead" station for "the black T-shirt crowd," to a legitimate entity in the market. In addition to the morning show being near the top of all primary demographics like 18- to 34-year olds and 25- to 54-year-old adults, male and female, "J.C. and The Morning Zoo" had inadvertently managed to pull in an astounding, unprecedented *eighty-two percent* of the teen audience!

One KSHE sales manager privately thanked me for putting his son through college.

The success, however, came at a price. At the time, I was trying to take advantage of every opportunity, every interview request, every personal appearance and as many sales calls as I could fit in. I was also doing my side job of entertainment reporting for KSDK, while maintaining the already grueling schedule of rising at five every morning, oftentimes after very little sleep. The result was that I was constantly sick. All that handshaking and close contact brought me face to face with every germ in the county. I missed the station Christmas party, which many chose to interpret as a hostile gesture. I also missed the "St. Louis City Ski" promotion the station had sponsored, which I was supposed to emcee. And when I get sick, I tend to get very sick.

So, when NBC offered two listeners and me the chance to be extras on what was the No.1 show in America at the time, *Miami Vice*, I said "yes," as much for the chance to be in a warm climate for a week as for anything else.

To my surprise, the listeners and I actually got to spend time with Don Johnson and Philip Michael Thomas at a party to honor the mayor of Miami. Johnson spoke of his Missouri roots; Thomas just spoke and spoke and spoke. The guest star that week was Frank Zappa who, during our interview, first hinted about the rising censorship problems within the music industry; a revelation that would bring us face to face again a few years later. The next day, I was again reminded of why I was never really interested in becoming an actor. We boarded a bus at 9 a.m., and around 9:30 p.m. we finally shot our scene. I ended up being on-camera for a total of four seconds.

By the time I returned to St. Louis I was sick again, and I was forced to miss our annual St. Patrick's Day live broadcast from Laclede's Landing. I could tell the station was not happy about my absence, and seemed suspicious that I might be feigning illness for some ulterior motive.

Convinced that things were getting out of hand and, no doubt, inspired by what the corporate lawyers said were newly threatened lawsuits, John Ulett, Don Johnson and I were pulled off the air one morning and flown to Indianapolis for a long, drawn-out "seminar" on slander, libel and corporate policy. Most of the droning seemed to roll off D.J.'s back, but I knew the lecture must have been mortifying to Ulett. Here was one of the most non-confrontational people I have ever known, being dragged through a humiliating episode simply because of his association with me. I felt as though I'd really let John down.

The suits made it abundantly clear we were not well liked. That I could live with. But it also was made abundantly clear we were not well respected. That I could not live with.

But I was also having problems with where the show was at, too.

The callers seemed divided into two camps about me: one side acted as though I was vermin, the other half seemed to think that anything I said or did was divinely inspired. Frankly, I wasn't comfortable with either camp. Dressing in army fatigues and partying in the parking lot of The Arena with "The KSHE Real Rock Army" before a rock concert was making me feel sillier and sillier. "The One-Hour Dirty Joke," once a fun feature of the morning show, was becoming infected with racial, homosexual and AIDS jokes.

And then there was the facility.

As you'll recall, the KSHE studios in Crestwood were nothing short of an embarrassment. I was trying to elevate the station's prominence with star bookings, and our in-studio guests, who were used to network television appearances and star treatment, couldn't conceal the "wait-until-I-get-my-hands-on-my-agent" look once they saw the inside of the building.

I had been asking about the rumors that the station would be moving, but was told that the station still hadn't reached a decision. Finally, in the late spring of 1986, KSHE announced it would be relocating to the Union Station Annex, sometime near the end of the year. I thought this was good news. I was wrong.

The move was still nearly seven months away. And even though every piece of ancient, broken-down equipment was going to be replaced in the new facility, it meant that management wasn't going to lift a finger to fix the old stuff, which was rapidly becoming more and more dysfunctional.

In July of 1986 I decided to take a few days off to re-charge. When I got back to work the following Monday morning, I found the facility in almost total disrepair. Almost everything I needed to do my job with in a professional manner—telephone, mixer, recorder, microphone and auxiliary piece of equipment—was broken or malfunctioning. My efforts to get the situation resolved via the proper channels had been ignored, and I truly felt that the station's failure to correct such egregious problems would destroy everything I had worked for. For the first hour of the show, I felt so emotional I thought I would burst into ears. Then I got angry. Finally, in a sort of peaceful resolve, I made a decision.

I explained the situation to the audience, and then gave out the phone number of Emmis Broadcasting's corporate office in Indianapolis. If the company wouldn't listen to me, maybe it would listen to our fans.

I only heard that they got "lots of calls" when they handed me my indefinite suspension notice the next day. But when my lawyer argued that there was no provision in the contract for a suspension, the situation became inflamed. Then, when Emmis' attorney called my boss at KSDK and, in an attempt at some sort of completely fallacious, legal hocus pocus, demanded he pull me off television too, we realized this was serious business.

Jerry Berger called daily for updates. A phony story a day surfaced about what had really happened and what was going to happen next. Finally, I instituted a "hotline" number, which Berger printed. For the next seventy-three days, the number generated roughly one thousand calls a day.

But those days off the air also generated a great deal of bad press, reinforcing the notion that I was difficult to work with. The suspension also resulted in many missed opportunities. One that still hurts involves one of my "Top Ten" favorite films of all time, *Planes, Trains and Automobiles.* The movie, starring Steve Martin and John Candy, was filmed in St. Louis in late 1986, while I was sidelined. When the director needed a radio voice for a scene in which Martin and Candy are driving northbound on I-55 in the middle of the night, the job went to KSHE's Al Hofer. Because of that scene, to this day, Al is my hero ... while at the same time I'd be lying if I didn't admit to being consumed by jealousy.

In the fall of 1986 I picked up the phone and called Program Director Rick Balis. After some initial skepticism, Rick agreed to meet me for lunch. I explained some things to him, he explained some things to me, and the announcement was made that I would return to KSHE for the final day of broadcasting from the "historic" Crestwood studios.

At a few minutes before 8 a.m. in the fall of 1986, I threw a switch that killed the power to the KSHE transmitter. John Ulett, Don Johnson and I walked a few hundred feet to a waiting helicopter, where we were flown to a landing pad a few blocks from Union Station. A white stretch limo drove us to the front entrance of the Annex where we got out, walked into the new studios, and threw another switch supplying power to the new facility. "Layla," by "Derek and the Dominoes," gushed out of the speakers. The table was set for us to begin a new chapter in KSHE history.

A month later I would be gone.

"I have enough money to last me the rest of my life. Unless, of course, I have to buy something."

—Comedian Henny Youngman

Chapter 14

When the station's draft of the new contract arrived in early November of 1986 the message was clear: Emmis wanted me to stay, but only if I would do exactly as they said. To underscore this point, all safeguards had been eradicated and all legal support pulled. If I got sued, I was on my own. Actually, let me correct that: If I got sued, the contract stated that I not only had to pay my own legal fees, I had to pay theirs as well.

Negotiations for a contract renewal began, but the writing was on the wall. Things were being taken out of the hands of John Beck and Rick Balis. Too much damage had been done.

But an incident that really hit hard was a giant "Welcome Back" cake delivered to me by some loyal listeners. I thanked them on the air and, as customary, had it taken down to the kitchen area where all the staff could enjoy it. I got hungry near the end of the show, and wandered down the hall during a record to grab a piece. It was a rude awakening.

Someone had taken a knife and gouged my name out of the cake.

There was no mistaking it. Someone from our own staff was sending—not just me, but everyone at the station—a hateful message.

The incident particularly upset me because I had always felt that in all my fights—over better facilities, more money, and even more respect—I was, in essence, fighting for everyone at the station. Salaries, conditions and opportunities had improved for all of us.

A huge, classic rock station in Chicago had been increasing the attractiveness of an offer for months. I had my lawyer call them and ask to formalize the offer. It was time to leave St. Louis. It was time to go home.

While all of this activity swirled, there was one diversion.

A still, relatively unknown movie director by the name of Taylor Hackford (who'd had a teensy bit of success with a film called *An Officer and a Gentleman* in 1982) had been contacted by Keith Richards of The Rolling Stones. In October of 1986, Hollywood descended upon the Fox Theatre for the making of, "Hail! Hail! Rock and Roll! A Tribute to Chuck Berry."

I got the call to be the evening's emcee, but I already knew this was going to be a tough experience. For one, tickets were sold for two separate crowds to witness the event; meaning, one crowd would watch for several hours, then another crowd would be brought in later in the night. Those purchasing tickets were under the mistaken impression that they were going to see a traditional "concert." But what they were actually going to see was a movie being made *about* a concert.

I did my best to explain this to the crowd when I took the stage, but to no avail. After reading a series of handwritten, congratulatory notes from music stars unable to attend (including Bob Dylan and Mick Jagger), I introduced the band, and the show began. Eric Clapton, Keith Richards and Chuck Berry each took the stage. But instead of allowing the performers to play a song all the way through, there were frequent starts and stops, including long gaps in which Hackford wandered the stage looking for perfect camera angles. Most of the crowd grew increasingly bored and irritated as the night dragged on.

Backstage the scene was volatile. Richards and Berry looked as though they were going to have to be forcibly kept apart before one of them took a Rickenbacker guitar across the teeth; Linda Ronstadt looked like she was desperate to be anywhere but here. Finally, around 1:30 a.m., I handed the announcing duties over to colleague, Drew Johnson, and headed home for about three hours of sleep.

Because of the demanding hours, I often worked on very little sleep. Unfortunately, this also meant that, on occasion, I went on the air with very little show preparation. One such morning, over the intro of the Pink Floyd song, "Another Brick in the Wall," which has long periods of helicopter sound effects, I improvised a bit, using the bullhorn I always kept at my side. (At KSHE, we were always jealous of stations that had a traffic reporter in a helicopter, so we often made fun of stations that did.) So with Pink Floyd playing in the background, it seemed perfectly logical that I would scream into the bullhorn as though I were KSD traffic-'copter pilot Allen Barklage reporting that the rotor blades had stopped and I was about to crash into the river. Truthfully, it was an inconsequential, throw-away bit. But the next morning, the incident was made into a front-page headline in the *Globe-Democrat.*

The paper, which had never missed an opportunity to take a swipe at me, claimed it had received dozens of calls complaining that "something should be done" to punish me for such a heinous, despicable act of bad taste. This, in turn, caused KSHE to get more complaint calls from readers who'd seen the story in the paper. I was told several clients had to be talked out of pulling their advertising from the station.

It was less than a week before Thanksgiving, and contract negotiations were going nowhere. On Tuesday I was called into John Beck's office and, in uncharacteristic fashion, was told I had to sign the new contract before midnight. I told John I couldn't do that.

Wednesday morning we had scheduled Hiram Bullock Jr., the bass player for David Letterman's band, to play in the studio. It was a great segment. When I got off the air, John and Rick told me I had done my last show for KSHE.

I emptied the contents of my cubicle into my car. Then I returned to the studio where I proceeded to take an electronic eraser to the hundreds of tape cartridges containing the themes, bits, drop-ins and comedy segments I had used to spice up the show. I left the building completely at ease with my decision. The next morning, the *Post-Dispatch* ran a front-page headline claiming, "KSHE Fires J.C. Corcoran." The headline and story couldn't have been more misleading. Though I had made the conscious decision to pass on what I considered to be a miserably insufficient contract, the *Post* characterized it as a "firing." I wasn't surprised, though. The local press never seemed to miss an opportunity to slam me, whether it was deserved or not.

The next morning KSHE General Manager John Beck and Program Director Rick Balis, two men I liked and respected and with whom I'd spent some of the most exciting, rewarding and memorable days of our mutual careers, went on the air. In a seventeen-minute-long, formal announcement, the men explained that the two sides had not been able to agree on a new contract, and that the J.C. Corcoran "era" at KSHE had come to an end.

"The man had a good heart," John concluded.

(I later learned that many listeners, including several friends of mine who had picked up the announcement in the middle, thought I had died.)

I left for Chicago to begin looking at houses; Jeff, in the meantime, stepped up negotiations with WCKG there. But shortly after the first of the year, a major shake-up took place in the corporate structure of the company that owned WCKG. Suddenly, Jeff was faced with a new set of managers who weren't thrilled with the juicy parts of the contract, which had taken months to negotiate. The situation began to sour, and Jeff suggested we explore other opportunities in St. Louis.

A week or so later Jeff called to tell me he'd received a return call from Gannett Radio, owners of KSD-FM.

He had also heard from Bob Hyland at KMOX.

Postscript: *It would be another six months before I would learn who was responsible for the fallout over my impersonation of KSD traffic-'copter pilot Allen Barklage in distress. I shouldn't have been surprised ... but I was.*

"Never assume you've seen the last of anything."
—Author Eudora Welty

Chapter 15

H ere we were. One Memorial Drive. We had pulled up to the secret rear gate, deposited into the back elevator for a quick flight up to the third floor, and swiftly ushered into the crystal-adorned, private office of Robert Hyland, vice-president and general manager of KMOX radio. It was all I could do to keep from laughing hysterically.

To say there were a few awkward silences in that first meeting would be like saying there were a few exciting plays during the Rams' Super Bowl season. Within the first two minutes, Hyland brought up the subject of the disparaging comments I'd made when his daughter was the VP Fair "queen." I calmly explained that I was sure she was a lovely woman, and that the joke was directed more at the event rather than the person ... or something like that. Though I thought that part of the discussion was over, I was surprised when he suggested that I "meet her some day."

What?!

Word spread quickly that I'd been seen in the building. That sighting, however, only served to intensify the interest from Gannett's KSD. My first meeting with KSD's general manager, Merrell Hansen, took place in her car in a remote corner of the parking lot of Chesterfield Mall. Merrell was a very bubbly, very short, round-faced, pretty blonde who looked as though she still had all of her baby fat. Unfortunately, her station was dribbling out Dionne Warwick and Captain & Tennille records so I couldn't imagine working there.

On the other hand, Hyland's idea was to put me on in the afternoon on then Top 40-formatted KHTR-FM, with an unspecified menu of assignments on KMOX. At one point during our discussion, Hyland asked how I planned to handle the issue of all the highly publicized bad blood that existed between us. I told him I wanted to diffuse it by referring to him on the air as "Uncle Bob." From the look I received, one would think I'd just told him he really *was* my uncle.

Though neither option seemed realistic, we continued to negotiate with KMOX/KHTR and KSD while waiting to see if either situation became more attractive. After four meetings in Hyland's office, we finally asked to see a contract. That request drew a peculiar response.

"I'm going to give you a list of names. You tell me what they all have in common," Hyland said. Then he proceeded to read off all the names of the KMOX on-air staff. "None of them have contracts," he concluded. Jeff and I nodded, and got on the elevator. I never saw Hyland again.

Then, in one of the great gambles of my professional career, I called Merrell and told her I'd made a decision; we'd be making an announcement in a few days. She immediately began protesting that this was not fair, and that she be given another opportunity to make a counter-proposal. Of course, the only decision I had made was to go to work for her; she just didn't know that.

A few days later Jeff called with KSD's final offer. It was absolutely outrageous: three years, no-cut, $50,000-a-year raises built-in, approval of co-hosts and, in addition to the contractual points, a promise to begin moving the station's format in a more hip, more rock-based direction.

I had just won the lottery.

I called John Ulett and offered him the opportunity to rejoin me at KSD. But John had been with KSHE for over a dozen years, and the decision was not easy for him. After weeks of meetings and negotiations, John finally agreed to jump to KSD for a sizable raise. A group of about ten of us gathered at John's attorney's office in Clayton. The Champagne was on ice and a copy of the contract was ready for John to sign. John was expected to arrive at 4 p.m.; the clock said 4:10, still no John. John's lawyer got a call; I saw him get up, and close the door.

John had gotten as far as putting all of his belongings in a box.

We were now less than two weeks from going on the air with a new morning show, and we had no co-host. Although I didn't know him very well, Joe "Mama Mason" and I had worked together a few times. Joe had been a substitute co-host when I was at KSHE, but he'd since fallen somewhat out of favor with the station and was no longer on the air every day. Joe said that he would be thrilled for the opportunity to work with me.

Since we wouldn't be paying Joe the kind of money we'd offered Ulett, it was decided we'd offer Don "D.J." Johnson the opportunity to rejoin us, too. *Post-Dispatch* television critic Eric Mink had begun contributing to KSD's morning show earlier in the year, and we all knew it was a wise move to keep him on.

And so it was that on May 11, 1987, that "J.C. and The Breakfast Club" was set to hit the airwaves of KSD. I remember thinking to myself, "Why didn't I just let KSHE play those Prince and Madonna records?"

But we hit two major snags before we got there. One came from St. Louis' television stations; the other, from "the friendliest stores in town."

"Doing the best at this moment puts you in the best place for the next moment."
—Talk Show Host Oprah Winfrey

Chapter 16

The motorcade of a half-dozen vehicles proceeded south on I-55 shortly after dawn on a late spring morning. The destination: Bonne Terre, Missouri, where the area's sand dunes would provide the setting for the new television commercial announcing my return to the St. Louis airwaves. A local advertising agency designed the spot to resemble a scene from the "road warrior" movies. The storyboard read as follows: *"J.C., dressed in a tattered, black, sleeveless T-shirt, black pants, boots and sunglasses emerges from over the top of a massive dune, surveys the bleak and barren landscape, then reaches into the sand and, in a broad motion, sweeps sand off the top of what's revealed as a radio control board, which then flickers dramatically and comes to life."*

Pretty cool, huh?

But the graphic and effects added in post-production would cause a major problem for this commercial. More about that later.

It would be almost two full months from the time I signed the new contract with KSD until I actually went on the air in May 1987. But as soon as the deal was made official in March, the station alerted Jerry Berger of the *Post-Dispatch*, who ran the story as the lead story in his Sunday column.

The next day KSD got a call from Schnucks' managerial office. The station was informed that the grocery chain was pulling **all** its advertising—in the neighborhood of $100,000—from KSD's commercial schedule. The announcement sent shock waves through the station, and throughout the local industry. The message was clear: The

Schnucks folks didn't like me.

KSD's management scrambled for answers, terrified there might be this same kind of reaction from other sponsors. Several sales executives grilled me on whether I'd ever made derogatory comments about Schnucks on the air. "Of course not," I said. "In fact, I do almost all my shopping there!"

A meeting was quickly thrown together. A dozen of KSD's highest-ranking executives accompanied me to the Schnucks' corporate headquarters in West County on a rainy, weekday afternoon. The plan was to dazzle the Schnucks people with my charming personality while itemizing the litany of charitable and community activities I had personally participated in and supported over the years. I also had to reassure them that the new show on KSD would be far less offensive than what we'd previously done on KSHE.

We were escorted into an enormous meeting room with a table the size of a swimming pool. The woman whose decision it was to chop us from their budget entered the room and took the seat at the head of the table. I swear the temperature in the room dropped twenty degrees. KSD's general manager made a very brief and carefully worded introductory statement, and then I began reading off my list of "achievements." I was about thirty seconds into the presentation (which included mention of the American Red Cross and the American Cancer Society, to name a few) when the woman pushed her chair back, looked at my boss and bit off the words, "I don't have time for this s**t."

It was a long drive back to the station.

Presumably, as part of a pre-emptive strategy, KSD's management decided to bring me along on their annual client outing. So, in March of 1987, still more than a month before I was to go on the air, I found myself on a plane bound for Pebble Beach. On board this flight had to be close to seventy-five representatives and their spouses from the city's largest and most-powerful businesses and advertising agencies. And I mean these were the *real* fat cats.

The point of these yearly station-sponsored trips is to schmooze the hell out of the station's biggest clients. In my case, the idea was to make them comfortable with the new show, and to convince them that the new direction the station would be taking would be good for business—especially *their* businesses, I might add. My brain is not big enough to fathom how much money the station spent that week. After all, this was one of America's most-exclusive, most-expensive golf resorts, and every imaginable expense was being picked up by KSD.

I golfed for the first time in my life the next morning. I remember being told by the other players that I had "a lot of natural ability." I also remember having to borrow some balls about halfway through the round, as I had lost all of mine.

It was on that trip that I first met John Craddock, aka, "Frank O. Pinion." At the time, he was doing the morning show at KUSA-AM, which was owned and operated by the same company as KSD, and had studios and offices across the hall. Frank received me about as well as Kathie Lee Gifford would be received at the Apollo Theater. I had a feeling that he would prove to be a problem for me in the future.

After my return from Pebble Beach, we got to work on the new television commercial. While standing on top of a sand dune in Missouri with a crew of over a dozen technicians and production people, I heard the unmistakable chopping sound of a helicopter above me. When I looked up, I saw it was Allen Barklage in the KSD/KUSA "Yellowcopter" (so-named because of its brightly painted, yellow coat). It turned out the director of the spot had asked Allen to fly above us in order to produce swirling, blowing sand, creating the effect of total desolation. All I could think about was the fatal accident on the set of the movie, *The Twilight Zone*, in which the same effect ended in the tragic death of two actors. Except, this time, I would be the fatality.

Allen flew me back to St. Louis after the shoot. It was the first opportunity I'd had to speak with him since signing onto KSD. Now, as you'll recall, I'd had a fascination with helicopters ever since my days as a kid practically living next to Midway Airport in Chicago. This news came as a delight to Allen. Then, we had a good laugh about the front-page story that had appeared in the *Globe-Democrat* the previous fall, in which I was vilified for simulating a crash of his aircraft. But Allen kept laughing.

"You know how that story got in the paper, don't you?" he asked. Evidently it was a rhetorical question, because Allen proceeded to tell me that the management of KSD—my new bosses—had staged the entire "protest" themselves. Allen, apparently consumed by a state of total hilarity, swung his head back and forth as we flew over South County. He even told me he'd been sitting in the general manager's office as the KSD staff deluged the switchboard of the paper with complaint calls about my on-air bit.

The next day, I walked into a department head meeting at the station and asked about Allen's claim. My query was met with waves of thunderous laughter. Not only did they own up to having manufactured the "community outcry," they bounced in their chairs like first-graders, giggling in glee at one another's personal memories of the fun. The meeting was punctuated by a story from former Big Red lineman Bob Rowe, then a sales manager with the station and a man with hands the size of toilet seats. Rowe posessed a low tolerance for smart-alecks like me, and recalled having to be physically restrained by his wife after seeing me in line at a movie theater in Chesterfield.

This was an odd group.

After weeks of preparation, "J.C. and The Breakfast Club" was about to go on the air. The television spot we had filmed in Bonne Terre was put through the final editing process, which included a "dissolve" from my "road warrior" sequence to a full-framed shot of electronic static for several seconds. The announcer then said; "*Beginning May 11th, St. Louis will become radioactive.*" No call-letters. No frequency. Nothing to indicate that it was a commercial for a radio station.

The television stations refused to air it.

Indirectly, this collective refusal worked to our benefit: the newspapers and news shows on TV quickly began running stories about the commercial. KSDK's John Pertzborn aired a two-minute piece featuring man-on-the-street interviews, which revealed the belief among viewers that the commercial was a warning a train containing nuclear waste might be coming through St. Louis. Finally, on Sunday night, May 10, 1987, KSD bought what's called a "roadblock" campaign (this meant the revised commercial would run on every St. Louis television station at exactly the same time—9:58 p.m., immediately prior to the news.) The cost for this kind of campaign is huge, but the guarantee is that everyone who has the TV on will see it. In this revised commercial, though, after the announcer delivered the "radioactive" line, a graphic with my name and new radio station appeared on the screen.

The next day, "J.C. and The Breakfast Club" with Joe "Mama Mason"; Don "D.J." Johnson; a relatively new sportscaster from Channel Five, Mike Bush; Allen Barklage; and Eric Mink debuted on 93.7 KSD. Judy Martin, a former intern of mine at Channel Five, would be added as our producer.

As a surprise, the station flew my parents and sister in from Chicago for the festivities. It looked as though we were on our way to something great.

Surprise, surprise.

Postscript: *Although we would go on to practically dominate our time slot for the next five years, Schnucks never bought a commercial on our show. To this day, I don't know why. Although it would take me nearly ten years, the supermarket chain and I now maintain a healthy relationship and its commercials air frequently on The Breakfast Club. And, thankfully, Bob Rowe and I proceeded to get along just fine.*

"Let your enemies know where you are and then don't **be** *there."*

—Comedian Chris Rock from *Dogma*

Chapter 17

O ne of the things I'm certain contributed to John Ulett choosing to pass on the opportunity to join us at KSD was the fact he was spooked by the station's music. Though the "adult contemporary" playlist had contained ample selections of Barry Manilow and Neil Diamond, a new program director from Atlanta quickly replaced that sludge with new songs from hipper artists like Steve Winwood and U2. However, because the sales staff was terrified the old audience might go away faster than the new audience would arrive (resulting in a ratings dive), management caved in, and a good chunk of the old music list remained on the air. Unfortunately, that strategy caused the station's identity to suffer greatly in our first year. The primary reason a station has a format is for consistency, and we had none at KSD.

Several of the disc jockeys from the old format were kept on, too. Since most of them didn't know the difference between REO and REM, this lack of knowledge came across on the air, crippling our credibility.

Gannett's president and vice-president of programming kept coming in from L.A. to complain that "Whitney Houston has the No. 1 song in the country and KSD isn't playing it!"

While all this was going on, Frank O. Pinion was causing a stink across the hall at KUSA-AM, an old-fashioned country music station that played songs with titles such as, "I Like Beer." In what I would classify as a textbook case of professional jealousy, Frank was very vocal about his view that the company had infected the building with my presence. He was even more outraged that the company was spending huge amounts of money on TV commercials, billboards and bus signs to promote us. Though he'd recently signed a new, multi-year contract, Frank walked in one day and quit, making no secret of why he was leaving.

Now, Frank was extremely popular with the sales staff, most of whom sold time for both KUSA and KSD. We weren't as popular as Frank for two simple reasons: Frank did the folksy, family-style "live endorsements," in which a sixty-second spot could often run about three or four minutes; a feature the sales staff naturally loved. Second, Frank and his people were more like the sales staff themselves. KUSA was the "family-values" group; we were the young renegades "playing all that awful music that's ruining KSD!"

Frank's departure turned the KSD sales staff's attitude toward us from resentful to downright hostile. General Manager Merrell Hansen did her best to rally the troops behind us but, on the rare occasions they did so, they did so begrudgingly.

(The station, incidentally, took Frank to court claiming breach of contract; evidently he found the right loophole, because the judge sided with him. Months later, Frank O. Pinion resurfaced at a low-powered FM country station.)

In the meantime, our new show hit the ground running. But we were about to face a series of challenges; many of which came from our competitors, and many of them of the legal variety.

The station wanted to portray us as more family friendly; as a result, we landed a Union Station promotion called "Scoops of Fun." This involved broadcasting over the course of a weekend from a giant, ice cream festival, complete with entertainment, which included an appearance by the "Steam Heat Dancers." But when KMOX chief Bob Hyland caught wind of our lineup, he canceled the group's involvement in the event. (He was able to do this since KMOX was sort of a tertiary level sponsor of the dancers.) In response to his move, I went on the air and announced that our event would go on fine without them, and besides, "It's common knowledge I've banged six of them anyhow."

A man identifying himself as the manager of the "Steam Heat Dancers," filed a million-dollar lawsuit against the station and me, claiming slander and alleging that my comments would expose the women to "public hatred" in the future. Over the course of the next two years, we would find Hyland's fingerprints all over the whole thing. The case was eventually settled out of court.

It's unusual for St. Louisans to have severe weather during their morning drive, but one particular morning when we were on the air, a major line of severe storms was pounding the area. Since this was before the days of readily available radar images, we called the National Weather Service office in St. Louis to ask for some information. However, the meteorologist who answered the phone said she didn't have time to talk to us because she had to go on the air on another radio station in a few minutes. When I pointed out the stupidity of that statement (considering the fact we were already on the air with her and that what she wanted to do with another station later was of no consequence to us), she got very snippy and indignant, then hung up. Then it dawned on me: Bob Hyland had somehow engineered a deal with the National Weather Service in St. Louis to prepare exclusive hourly reports for KMOX, and, clearly, we has just been blown off by a woman who was preparing a bulletin for them. Apparently our listeners could just get sucked into a tornado as long as she got on KMOX.

As you might expect, I ranted and railed about someone withholding the weather forecast, and finally referred to the woman as a ... (gasp!) ... "bitch." She threatened to sue, but never did. This incident did lead, however, to an official policy change, effected by the government, which bars the NWS from providing any one station with "personalized" weather reports.

It was at about this time that St. Louis was abuzz with the details of the bizarre murder case of Julia Bullock at the hands of her husband, Dennis. The couple had met through a *Riverfront Times* personal ad and, after marrying, had moved to a house in West County. After an allegedly "rough sex" episode, Dennis claimed to have accidentally killed his wife, and then set the place on fire to conceal the evidence. One morning on the air, I wondered whether Julia Bullock had had her bridal registry at Central Hardware.

Central Hardware pulled its advertising from the station the following day.

OK. That one was my fault.

The Fourth of July weekend was approaching, and I knew that KSD had always participated in the annual Veiled Prophet Fair. This particular year KSD had made arrangements, in conjunction with Bi-State and the St. Louis area Venture stores, for me, along with a group of contest winners, to broadcast live from a Bi-State bus, which would travel along the parade route.

I was to meet the group around 4 p.m. at the parade start-point, on the western edge of downtown. When I stopped at the station in Creve Coeur around 3 p.m. to make one last check on the technical plans, however, I was met with grim faces. I was completely shocked to learn that KSD's management team had been on the phone for most of the day, trying to smooth out the effects of a threat from VP Fair officials that "J.C. Corcoran will be arrested if he tries to broadcast from this parade."

Arrested? For *what*?

Allyn Glaub, a spokesman for the VP Fair, told the *Post-Dispatch* that parade organizers had been upset with me because, in 1985, I'd offered $500 to anyone who could "unveil" the identity of the Veiled Prophet. As I stood there with my jaw on the floor, I had to think hard to remember the incident. The fact that I was barely able to recall having made the comment *as a joke* two years earlier, just made this situation that much more ludicrous.

For a few minutes, there was actually some discussion about letting them arrest me. (Imagine the publicity!) As *Post-Dispatch* readers would learn the following morning, that discussion quickly ended when our engineers and promotion staff called from the parade site and informed us that VP Fair officials, along with officers from the St. Louis Police Department, had just "raided" the bus we were to have broadcast from. In Gestapo-like fashion, officials and police had ordered everyone off the bus, removed roughly $15,000 worth of broadcast equipment, transmitters, speakers and promotion signage, and repeated the threat that I would be arrested if I so much as attempted to *board* the bus. Then they threatened to arrest KSD Chief Engineer Dave Obergoenner, Promotion Director Cathy Kelly and Promotions intern Anne Marie Todt. Cathy was the daughter of beloved St. Louis Blues announcer, Dan Kelly, and Anne Marie was the daughter of prominent Clayton attorney, Chuck Todt.

Might *that* have made for an interesting courtroom.

To add insult to injury, Dave Obergoenner informed us that VP Fair officials wanted the contest winners off the bus so that it could be used to ferry other VP officials to another location. The winners refused to get off. Even more insane was the insistence by fair officials that they could do whatever they wanted since this was "a private parade."

For weeks we had been announcing the plans for a live broadcast from the parade, and now it was just hours before the start. Merrell Hansen emerged from her office with a surprisingly brilliant-but-simple plan. We still had a separate, portable, wireless microphone unit available, and if I was simply standing there with the unit on public property, there probably wouldn't be a thing anyone could do to me. As an extra precaution, Merrell hired a three-man videotape crew to record every breath of my two-hour broadcast (I stood on a public street corner along Broadway), just in case some sort of bogus claim was made at a later date.

That Bi-State bus carrying our contest winners passed by me near the end of the parade and broadcast. Although they cheered supportively, I could see that every trace of KSD's presence, including a life-sized cardboard cut-out of me, had been stripped away. When the parade was over, Merrell, along with the camera crew, followed me all the way to my car.

I drove home asking myself, *What is going on in this town?*

On July 8, 1987, Bill McClellan, in a column entitled, "Daughter of a Knave May Never Be Queen," wrote in the *Post-Dispatch*:

'Unfortunately, I haven't always been so supportive of the Veiled Prophet ball. I certainly would never encourage anyone to rip the sheet off of the Veiled Prophet, and I wouldn't condone a disc jockey encouraging people to do it. But hey, bygones should be bygones. A disc jockey ought to be able to cover a public event. At any rate, if the VP people are going to hold grudges, then I'm afraid my daughter will never be queen. I tried to explain that to her as we drank our hot chocolate. Your dad has ruined your chances, I told her. "I don't want to be a queen, dummy," she said.'

In retrospect, KSD General Manager Merrell Hansen made a tough call that day. As a community leader and operator of a large mainstream broadcast facility, she could have easily played the situation from a position of political expediency. Instead, she stood up to people who were wrong and fought for what was right. The short, attractive blonde with the big eyes outfoxed the big, tough, mean boys that day.

The Cardinals were now making their second run at the playoffs in two years. Coming from Chicago, this was just incredible to me. I'd heard a funny phrase on an episode of *Cheers*, in which Shelly Long referred to someone as "pond scum," so I'd been applying that label to the hated New York Mets every opportunity I could get for well over a year. One night on an edition of "Viewer Mail" on *Late Night with David Letterman*, Dave read a letter from a St. Louis fan named Gary Brown. (And, no, contrary to popular, revisionist history it was not written by the late Gary "Records" Brown of KGLD fame.) In the letter Brown asked a silly question about Letterman's eyebrows and included the postscript, "The Mets are pond scum!" As Dave went on to explain the difference between pond scum and the Mets (using an elaborate series of charts and laboratory information), I could hardly believe what I was seeing. I was looking at something on national television that I had actually started. I knew come Monday, everybody would be talking about it.

I often played the audio of the segment on the air, but it wasn't until the Mets came to Busch Stadium for a three-game series against the Cardinals in July 1987 that KSD's promotion director, Cathy Kelly, thought of a brilliant way to capitalize on it.

Cards second-baseman Tom Herr stepped to the plate in the first inning, but the usual, enthusiastic reception he got from the crowd was accompanied by an odd murmur throughout the park. Herr took ball one, but the murmur continued, even increasing in volume. Herr stepped out of the batter's box and glanced skyward; announcers Ken Wilson and Al Hrabosky on the Cards Cable Network noted there was something in the sky. The next pitch was in the dirt, as the crowd of fifty thousand began cheering at a deafening roar.

Overhead was a plane dragging a banner that read, "93.7 KSD. J.C. SAYS THE METS ARE POND SCUM!" In addition, KSD had either sold and/or distributed a whopping sixteen thousand T-shirts bearing the phrase.

It was a good fifteen minutes before the crowd returned to normal. It was also about that time that Nancy McElroy, the adorable media relations rep for the Cardinals, showed up at my seat in the loge section behind home plate. She tapped me on the shoulder and said, "Dal would like to see you. Right *now*."

Uh-oh.

I was escorted into the bowels of Busch Stadium and into the office of Cardinals General Manager Dal Maxvill. He was sitting behind his desk with clearly an unhappy look on his face. His anger quickly softened to one of practical resolve as he explained that he'd just come from the Mets' dugout where he'd delivered a formal apology to the boys from the Big Apple. "Can you help me out, J.C.?" he asked. "We love your enthusiasm, but is there a way you can channel it into something more positive from now on?"

Dal Maxvill earned my unwavering respect that night. He could have taken my head off but, instead, he was a complete gentleman. We spoke for a few more minutes, shook hands, and then I just skipped the rest of the game and went home. I was feeling a little embarrassed and a little charged-up at the same time. I knew the stunt was a major hit, but had I sacrificed too much?

For the record, each encounter I had with Dal Maxvill—up to his departure from St. Louis several years ago—was more pleasant than the last. His group of four and my group of six ended up one table apart at a restaurant in St. Petersburg Beach at spring training a few years after the banner "pond scum" night. He called us over, talked with us for over an hour, and then picked up the tab for the entire bunch. I remember thinking that you just never know where your next friendship will come from.

But it also can be said that you just never know where your next enemy will come from, either.

After several on-air auditions produced miserable results, KSHE had brought in the morning team of "Mitchell, McCain and Buttery" from Atlanta to fill the hole my departure had left. Together with John Ulett, these were the guys who were going to try to stop KSD's momentum. Suddenly, all of the nice things KSHE's management had said about me seemed to have been made contingent upon my leaving St. Louis. Now that I was definitely staying, the kind words quickly turned ugly.

An all-out competitive battle between my new station and the old would be one thing, but early signs proved that this contest would disintegrate into something much creepier. At KSD, I was using many of the standard bits I had once used on KSHE, and the first challenge by KSHE's lawyers was over "Screen Test," a daily trivia contest I'd been doing since my days in Buffalo. Next, the lawyers went after "Wuh-Shu-Want," a rapid-fire phone segment. Then—unbelievably—they challenged my use of "Partytown," the signature feature I'd created for the show. All I seemed to be doing was sitting in meetings with lawyers, which, I was sure, was precisely where KSHE wanted me to be. Soon there were legal battles over my use of interview segments I'd recorded while under contract at KSHE, followed by leaflets distributed to advertisers, agencies and newsrooms, comparing KSD's ratings "before and after J.C.," and allegedly proving my new show was already considered a failure. The topper was a tape that KSHE's sales department put together, featuring all our mistakes, flubs, off-color humor and other out-of-context segments. The piece, all neatly edited and distributed around town, was specifically designed to make our show appear as unattractive as possible.

Copies of an in-house newsletter compiled by KSHE's marketing department fell into our hands and, for the first time, we saw just how personal the battle had become. Photos of Merrell Hansen and I had been mutilated and awkwardly pasted together, with ugly captions at the bottom. At a Westport comedy show I was emceeing featuring Dennis Miller and Dana Carvey, KSHE staffers stood outside the entrance handing out T-shirts and merchandise carrying their logo. KSHE then claimed to have a struck an exclusive deal with the Funnybone Comedy Club; their intent was to block our access to comedians playing that venue.

KSHE's deal with the comedy club was particularly annoying, since I'd made comedy a staple of the new show. After all, KSHE had a twenty-year relationship with the record companies and concert promoters, which virtually guaranteed its "ownership" of the local rock music scene. I intended to make comedy and entertainment our "rock," and if KSHE were successful in blocking my access to it, it would have made things difficult.

What KSHE forgot, however, was the television angle I still had via my duties at KSDK. So to get around the roadblock, I simply recorded the interviews I did for television and ran the audio on radio the following day. Finally, when KSHE's people tried to interfere with *Saturday Night Live's* Kevin Nealon and A. Whitney Brown's scheduled television interviews with me on Channel Five, the entire thing blew up in KSHE's faces. They had clearly overstepped their bounds as several high-powered New York agents, network reps and genuinely pissed-off, nationally-known comedians were more than eager to inform them.

I never had that problem again.

We quickly threw together the first of what would be our annual trips to the Cubs-Cardinals weekend in Chicago. The Redbirds appeared to be on a path that might take them to the playoffs, so we figured a lot of people would want to win trips to join us. I was familiar with a little bar at Waveland and Sheffield across from the Wrigley Field scoreboard called "Murphy's Bleachers," and made arrangements to rent the huge, open area on the roof. From the rooftop, we could look down over the open courtyard, and it seemed an ideal place to do the show. We only had a few weeks to plan the promotion, and quickly realized it would be impossible to buy tickets for thirty winners covering a three-game series. Instead, our prize package included airfare, a room at the team's hotel, and thirty bucks per person. The thirty dollars each winner received could be used toward the purchase of tickets from one of the many scalpers found at the ballpark on game day.

KSHE, still up to its old dirty tricks, sent packages to the winners' hotel in Chicago containing free tickets to a Cardinal home game and a letter of apology for our failure to provide tickets to the Cardinal/Cub game. Luckily, our support staff nabbed the packages before they made it to our winners.

But KSHE's dirty tricks didn't stop there. As the crowd cheered and sang along with "Partytown" at the end of our Saturday broadcast from Murphy's, a half-dozen kids hired by KSHE tossed dozens of KSHE T-shirts to our crowd.

I'd had enough.

I ran down the stairs into the crowd and chased one of the kids off the property, and, in one of the very few, semi-violent acts of my life, kicked him squarely in the tailbone every few feet of the chase. Moments later the cops showed up, looking as though they might be searching for someone. Someone in particular … like … oh … maybe **ME**?

I knew enough about the Chicago police to know I didn't want any part of *this* scene, so I quickly took off my shirt, put on a hat and disappeared into the huge crowd. But not before I saw our marketing director in a heated discussion with one of Chicago's finest, which ended with the cop whacking the marketing director across the face.

When we got back to St. Louis on Monday, I called a meeting with our station's management team. I was adamant that they take the necessary steps to ensure our safety, and emphasized that it was their responsibility to keep us from being pushed around by KSHE kooks and cops alike.

We traveled with the Cardinals through the 1987 playoffs against San Francisco, as well as the World Series against the Minnesota Twins. Our ratings were steadily rising, the show was sounding good, and I was making lots of money. I moved into a much larger house in Chesterfield and built a swimming pool.

We got some breaks early in our first eighteen months at KSD. *Wheel of Fortune* had become the hottest show in television, with well over forty million viewers a night. In St. Louis, nearly half the television sets in use were tuned to the hit show. I had gotten to know Vanna White on my trip to L.A. several months earlier when I was doing a five-part series on KSDK-TV. So when she went on a national tour to promote her book, *Vanna Speaks*, I had no problems booking her for an in-studio interview. It was a **very** big deal at the time.

Mike Bush also was making an invaluable contribution to the show. Even today, Mike gives credit for his popularity with St. Louisans to the time he spent on our show. Although he was on a St. Louis' top-rated news station, it was doing the "J.C. and The Breakfast Club" show that allowed him to bring the fun-loving side of his personality to the people of St. Louis and, in return, receive a loyal following.

Mike also was the subject of one of the most memorable stunts in the show's history.

Since it would have been impractical to expect Mike to come to the radio station each morning, a broadcast line was installed in his basement. There he would turn on a small power supply, put on a pair of headphones and perform what was referred to as "Sports in My Shorts," so-named because he often sat there in his underwear.

In the summer of 1988, we concocted a plan to surprise him on his birthday by doing the show in his basement. Mike's wife, Claudia, left the basement door unlocked the night before and, at 3 a.m., our engineers slipped in noiselessly to set up. One by one we arrived at the house, parking around the corner and tip-toeing in through the rear entrance.

The whole idea of what we had done, coupled with the knowledge that Mike was asleep two floors above us, struck us all at once at 6 a.m. when we went on the air. Listeners were treated to a case of giggles neither heard before—nor since—on the airwaves.

It seemed there was a newspaper or television story on us every two weeks. The combination of being on a top-rated morning show and the number one television news station meant people couldn't avoid seeing me. Fearing over-saturation in the market, I actually began to cut back on outside projects. There was no sense in getting people sick of me faster than was necessary!

Wanting to stay out of the news, though, can sometimes be more difficult than you'd think.

In what was clearly intended as a publicity stunt, Y98 delivered a press release to the *Post-Dispatch* mourning the passing of a frequent contributor to Guy Phillips' morning show. One problem: The contributor was nothing more than a character-voice performed by Phillips. An alert staffer at the paper called a representative of the station to try to clear things up, but was allegedly told that it was **not** a phony story, and the so-called contributor was for real.

The *Post-Dispatch* ran the story. Guy Phillips and the gang at Y98 just about busted a gut on the air.

Needless to say, when the managers at the paper realized they'd been hoodwinked, they issued a scathing follow-up to the story. Unbelievably, in the August 1, 1990, edition of the *Post*, Y98's general manager, Karen Carroll, defended the prank as harmless "theatre of the mind." Of course, most of us at KSD relished the idea of Carroll finally receiving her due. For years she'd been authorizing the practice of taping us at KSD, extracting the roughest examples of language on the show, then editing long strings of these out-of-context remarks together and sending the tapes to advertisers and agencies hoping they would cancel their commercials.

The very thought of having her backed into a corner put us in a nearly giddy state as we read the *Post* article on the air. We continued to embellish the story with crude comments ranging from suspicions of alleged plastic surgery to the even sillier notion of a possible sexchange operation, laughing hysterically and punctuating each joke with a rim shot.

Three months later, Carroll filed a multi-million dollar slander suit against Joe Mason, KSD and me. My repeated efforts to get a call through to Carroll to calm her down were unsuccessful, and the story was splashed all over the local media. One day when I arrived at Channel Five, Karen Foss asked to meet me in the station's conference room where she proceeded to take my head off over the incident. When she was finished, I gave her a quick rundown of her pal's long-running, dirty tricks campaign against not only me and KSD, but against a small handful of other St. Louis stations; something that, if the look on her face was any indication, she had been blissfully unaware of. Our little meeting seemed to end in a draw, and Karen Foss and I never had much to say to each other after that.

This abundance of negative energy, however, helped serve a purpose: I became much more focused on what I was doing. After all, I figured if I let my work slide, then people would think that their back-stabbing nonsense was working.

I'd been asking KSD's management for a day and a half of time on the station to try an idea I'd been working on for a couple years. I wanted to see how much food and money we could raise if we stayed on the air for thirty hours straight a few days before Christmas.

I had my reasons for this request, which dated back to my childhood:

It was an unusually warm Christmas Eve in Chicago. I was about ten years old at the time, and riding my "Stingray" bicycle (complete with banana seat and sissy bar) through a friend's neighborhood. A frail, old man poked his head out from behind a screen door, clearly attempting to get my attention. As I slowed down, with a thick, foreign accent he mumbled the word, "aspirin." The next time he made his request, he held out his hand, which contained a few dollar bills. I just sat there looking at him. Then I rode off.

I'm still haunted by this memory. Was he sick? Was his wife sick, and he was unable to leave her? Maybe he scared me. Maybe I was just a stupid, little kid. But, deep down, I think I behaved like a selfish little creep that day. And I later vowed that, if given the chance, I would try to help people during the holidays. I hoped that by helping others at this time I could erase this awful memory, which I had been carrying around for so many years.

The Salvation Army seemed to be the organization that helps those who need help the most. My radio idol in the 1970s, Larry Lujack of WLS in Chicago, had once asked his listeners to donate to the Salvation Army. The Salvation Army appeared to have the lowest amount of administrative cost, and their officials seemed completely dedicated to their cause. I even liked hearing their clanging bell outside Schnucks and their band playing in the mall; hearing those sounds meant Christmas was on its way.

The Saturday before Christmas 1987, we staged the first annual "Food and Cash Salvation Bash" at West County Center. At the end of the thirty-hour broadcast, which featured pro athletes, area dignitaries and several celebrities, we'd raised almost $25,000 and six tons of food. Memorable highlights of the event included performances by local musician and broadcaster Ross Gentile, as well as a late-night accordion performance by Channel Five meteorologist Bob Richards. At the time, I couldn't possibly have foreseen the heights we'd reach in future "Food and Cash" bashes.

After another disappointing season of Cardinal football, springtime meant another week of broadcasts from St. Petersburg with the baseball Cardinals, still stinging from their World Series defeat at the hands of the Minnesota Twins.

When we got back to St. Louis, the news was waiting for us.

The Arbitron ratings for the previous three-month period indicated a forty-seven percent increase in KSD's morning drive numbers from the previous year. "J.C. and The Breakfast Club" had risen to the No. 2 spot in the market in our target demographic of 25- to 54-year-old adults. It was the first time in years that KSHE had been knocked off.

To put it in simple terms, we won. It took less than a year to beat our main competitor. A story in the paper read, "J.C. Corcoran must be a happy guy as he tells his former bosses, 'I told you so'."

A few weeks later my phone rang.

It was an old buddy from Washington, D.C.

It was "The Smash."

Postscript: *"Mitchell, McCain and Buttery," my replacements on KSHE, learned an important lesson about broadcasting that year. Although they'd been a formidable entity in Atlanta, that reputation meant nothing here. Apparently, they had fallen into the trap of having believed their own press releases.*

"No society can long endure that has abandoned its ideals."

—Performer Steve Allen

Chapter 18

Rumors had been circulating for weeks that KSHE was about to make a change in their morning show. Asher Benrubi, aka, "The Smash," having grown up in Indianapolis, as well as having had a long radio career there, was well known by the Emmis Broadcasting people headquartered there. Given this corporate recognition, it wasn't hard to imagine why the "Smash" was invited to work at KSHE in St. Louis. We two friends would soon be pitted against each other.

Because of the incredible acrimony existing between the two stations, I voiced my concerns to "Smash." I told him that the Emmis' folks would make it so uncomfortable for him to remain on good terms with me, that we'd end up enemies, somehow. In his trademark, gravel-scarred voice he said, "We been friends too long, man. We been friends too long."

The "Smash" took that morning-drive slot at KSHE.

Three months later we were no longer speaking.

Predictably, KSHE's people lit a fire under Rob Buttery who had been kept on their show as the third wheel. His attacks against me became more personal, more vicious and more frequent in number. Clearly, the KSHE people banked on the idea that I wouldn't fire back because of my friendship with "Smash." But "Smash" was allowing it. And I considered *that* a violation of our friendship.

While that battle continued to brew, another new one was starting up between us and KMOX. Because of KSD's location—just miles from Lambert International near the intersection of Olive and

Lindbergh—the FAA required that traffic reporter, Allen Barklage, gain clearance from the airport control tower every time he wanted to take off from the small field directly behind the station. Irritated by what was often a lengthy wait, on occasion, Allen would simply take off without getting clearance. This lapse could cause problems for Allen, since all communication between pilots and the Lambert tower can be monitored by anyone in the area who's operating an aircraft.

There was no love lost between Allen and KMOX traffic reporter Don Miller. Allen characterized Miller as a "sandbag," the industry term for a traffic reporter who is flown by a helicopter pilot, as opposed to Allen, who reported traffic while flying his own 'copter. In fact, Allen had piloted Miller for a period of time before taking over reporting duties for KSD and KUSA, and often ridiculed Miller about his propensity to smack his lips annoyingly throughout his reports.

Miller, of course, thought his competitor was a hotshot. Allen was a decorated war hero, having served two tours of duty in Vietnam. There was also a highly publicized incident involving Allen in 1978, in which Allen was hijacked and forced at gunpoint to fly to an Illinois prison yard for an attempted pick-up of a prisoner. Fearing he'd be killed, either by prison guards or by the hijacker once the break was successful, Allen let go of the controls, wrested the gun from the woman who'd had it pointed at his head, then shot and killed her. After regaining control, Allen safely landed the helicopter in a field next to the prison.

Of course, Allen would go on to use his helicopter to fish several attempted suicide cases out of the Mississippi River over the next few years, and he rarely went more than a week without a speaking engagement at one of the area's schools.

On the other hand, Miller's most publicized incident occurred when he and his pilot forgot to perform a somewhat necessary, pre-flight procedure one day. At the end of each day's flying, two large "shoes" are placed on top of the front part of the helicopter's landing skids in order to secure it and keep it from blowing around in the event of an overnight storm. On this particular morning the pair failed to remove those shoes. Now, you don't have to have a degree in physics to visualize what happened at take-off. Of course, the pilot attempted to lift off the ground, at which point the tail end of the chopper flew up and the aircraft flipped completely over and into the river. Nobody was hurt, but an embarrassed Miller and pilot had some explaining to do.

Miller was the stodgy, old, retired cop. Allen was the young buck. It's the stuff of fierce competition.

One day I heard Allen had had his aviation license suspended for thirty days. Immediate allegations surfaced that KMOX's Miller had to have been involved somehow. In a Jerry Berger column in the *Post-Dispatch*, Miller vehemently denied having anything to do with it. We suspected otherwise.

It took a few months, but one day the letter landed on my desk. It was a single-spaced, poorly-typed, one-page letter to the FAA, authored and signed by Don Miller that itemized the dates and times Allen allegedly committed the infractions. On the day Allen's suspension ended, I took particular glee in reading that letter on the air.

Meanwhile, KSHE's good ol' Rob Buttery had dug all the way back to my Buffalo days to try to smear me. His new on-air claim was that I'd routinely gone on the air drunk.

I was at a crucial point. This stuff had nothing to do with some dumb radio war. This was personal.

I delivered a letter to KSHE asking General Manager John Beck, Program Director Rick Balis, and "Smash" to meet me at Union Station for an attempt at some sort of truce. They never showed. Feeling that my back was against the wall, I went on an unbridled offensive.

KSHE was in desperate need of a victory. This desperation led to a misguided effort to try to win *Rolling Stone* magazine's annual reader's poll award for "Radio Station of the Year."

We'd been hearing rumors that KSHE employees had purchased vast quantities of the magazine containing the ballots and filling them out themselves. In February of 1988, a triumphant KSHE staff appeared on the cover of *Rolling Stone* above the banner, "Station of the Year." But before we could—or needed-to do anything about the deceit, the *Post-Dispatch*, *Associated Press* and other news sources came down on KSHE for stuffing the ballot boxes. In the March 8, 1988, edition of the *Post-Dispatch*, KSHE General Manager John Beck admitted that "between eight hundred and one thousand ballots had been filled out by KSHE employees." Of course, Beck played down the episode.

(Interestingly, a year later, KSHE repeated the effort, stuffing the ballot box in the annual *Riverfront Times'* reader's poll. The result was an intern at KSHE being named St. Louis Radio Personality of the Year.)

But I thought one more shot at them might be worthwhile.

For the hard rock KSHE audience, nothing was more hated than disco and, for quite a while, I'd had a tape of a very brief chapter in Smash's career in Indianapolis radio when he had hosted a disco show. I knew it would cause a great deal of embarrassment to "Smash" were I to play it on KSD, so that's precisely what I did. We'd also heard detailed accounts of serious marital problems involving one of KSHE's top managers, including one particularly unattractive, public incident. I told the story on the air and named names.

Over the course of the next, few weeks I unloaded everything I had on anyone who was part of KSHE's operation. One morning "Smash" addressed the situation and, more importantly, addressed me personally. "You should be ashamed of yourself," he said repeatedly.

Though I strongly felt I wasn't the one who started this in the first place, I knew "Smash" was right. Looking back, returning a barrage of vicious, personal attacks against former friends, as well as innocent people, is something I consider to be the worst decision of my professional career. It hurt too many people, most of all me.

"It's more fun than humans should be allowed to have."
—Talk Show Host David Letterman

Chapter 19

I t *seemed* like a good idea.

One of David Letterman's goofy writers decided to set up a live camera at an airport luggage carousel and watch travelers claim their belongings. When too much red tape ruled out the New York facilities, unbelievably, we learned the camera would be set up at St. Louis Lambert International Airport.

I called my KSDK special projects producer, Ava Ehrlich, and reminded her that Letterman's show was taped from 4:30 to 5:30 p.m. St. Louis time. This meant that the taping at Lambert would be going on during Channel Five's early news. Wouldn't it be fun to go live from the airport and show our viewers a preview of what they'd be seeing on national TV later that night?

Wouldn't it?

My cameraman set up a few yards from the carousel so that the lively crowd of Letterman fans that had gathered for the extravaganza would be seen in the background when I did my report. The plan was for Dick Ford and Deanne Lane to toss it to me at Lambert, at which time I'd have the cameraman widen his shot to include the crowd, to be followed by an interview I'd recorded with *Late Night* writer, Fred Graver, earlier in the day. Then we'd cut back to me for a quick wrap and toss back to the studio.

Seconds before our live shot was to begin, my cameraman turned his bright, television light on and I started my delivery. At that very moment, I sensed commotion over my shoulder. The next thing I knew, the crowd seemed to be moving in my direction and ***another*** television camera and light were trained on me. Hanging on the second cameraman's belt was a speaker from which David Letterman was addressing me. (Keep in mind that all of this was going on as I was delivering my story to the Channel Five audience in St. Louis.)

Because of the total chaos, I was only able to catch parts of what Letterman was saying to me, but I remember hearing lots of laughter and applause from Dave's audience. I tried to answer his questions as best I could, but I had my own earpiece in, which was providing me with audio from the monitor and cues from the Channel Five producer back at the station.

When the whole thing was over I asked Letterman's writer what that was all about. "Oh, we just wanted to see what would happen and which camera you would play to," he responded.

But when *Late Night with David Letterman* aired that night, I saw something entirely different.

"When we knew we were going to be doing the segment from St. Louis, we called our affiliate there, KSDK-TV, and asked if they could spare a man or a woman from the station to sort of help out, and they told us, 'Well ... I don't think so.' (Audience boos loudly.) "And now, now it turns out they have a camera crew and reporter there ... oh ... this guy! This guy!"

The national television audience then got to see Letterman's camera sneak up on me from behind as Dave launched a barrage of insults and snide remarks my way. Not being able to hear much of what he was saying, I just stood there, grinning, which made me look like even more of a complete idiot.

"That's OK," he concluded. "Just go back to your little puppet show." (Loud cheering, laughter and applause from the audience.)

It wasn't until weeks later that I learned the real story behind Letterman's behavior.

Channel Five General Manager Bill Bolster was an enormous, larger-than-life character who had taken a last-place television station and converted it into not just the number-one station in St. Louis, but the top-rated NBC affiliate in the nation. "Shy" was not a word normally connected to the name Bill Bolster. Bill was a hog farmer from Iowa and proud of it!

One controversial move he had made was to tape-delay *Late Night with David Letterman* by one-half hour. By inserting locally originated programming into the 11:30 to midnight slot, the station could run its own commercials, and generate tons of additional revenue each year. But, as you might expect, the tactic was unpopular with NBC, which wanted Letterman to immediately follow Johnny Carson (as god had intended). As upset as NBC was with the set-up, Letterman was even more so.

So when Letterman's people called KSDK with the idea of asking for some assistance with the live-shot from Lambert, something went terribly wrong. I had heard from executives at the television station that Bolster and Letterman ended up in an allegedly heated exchange, even going so far as insulting each other's educational background. At the heart of the matter was Letterman's objection to the program being tape-delayed; Bolster, I'm sure, wondered why he should bear the expense and responsibility for something the network could do itself.

Needless to say, that night at Lambert, Letterman saw red. I was caught in the crossfire or, simply put, I was in the wrong place at the wrong time.

Later that same year I had a much more successful appearance on national TV. But it came at a terribly expensive price.

I've long been of the opinion that all televangelists are crooks. I must also confess to having a peculiar fascination with them. As early as 1980, I can recall getting up early on Sunday mornings to watch guys like Jerry Falwell, Ernest Angley and, later, Benny Hinn. And, of course, the *PTL Club* with Jim and Tammy Faye Bakker. The idea that people would willingly follow and, subsequently, turn their hard-earned money over to these guys was beyond my comprehension.

At the same time, the Reagan administration's conservative appointees to the FCC had reached the point of obsession with the state of wacky, unrestrained and otherwise off-the-wall radio shows. Consequently, they had been handing out fines like our Rock Hill police hand out speeding tickets. Under right-wing pressure from the likes of Jerry Falwell and Mississippi's Reverend Donald Wildmon, the United States government was handing fines out to the country's biggest, most-successful radio personalities. If an on-air discussion got a little racy, "Ed Meese and his mind police" would just have to ring you up.

My belief was government had the whole thing backward. The "Morning Zoo" shows weren't hurting anybody. Televangelists were.

So when the PTL scandal broke and Bakker's involvement with church secretary, Jessica Hahn, became the talk of the nation, I took particular glee in knowing I'd been onto this guy long beforehand. It's important to recall that Bakker was still on the air and scooping up loot long after the scandal was reported. His repeated denials of any wrongdoing were being seen on *Nightline*, the evening news programs and CNN. Tammy was continuing to stand by her man, and it was looking as though the Bakkers were hoping to weather the storm.

As the media descended upon Jessica Hahn, a critical eye turned toward her. Was the sex consensual? Did she seduce him? Was it all a set-up from the beginning? As the world waited to hear who was the liar in this scenario, Hahn negotiated a deal to tell her story and to be featured in a pictorial.

Joe "Mama Mason" and I had a long-standing relationship with some of the more connected people at *Playboy* in Chicago. This fortuitously allowed us (albeit very clandestined means) to have an advance copy of the Jessica Hahn interview issue delivered to the station days before it was to be released to the public. We had been told the piece would contain shocking, new allegations, but I didn't have time to read the interview before I was to go on the air. I had just begun reading excerpts aloud when it became apparent that Hahn was alleging Bakker had raped her and PTL money may have been illegally used in an attempt to silence her. Though there was no profanity in the detailed account Hahn gave the *Playboy* interviewer, the language she used to describe one specific moment of their sexual encounter was very explicit.

I had a decision to make on the spot. We had a legitimate news story in our hands, and in it, a new claim—that a rape had been committed—dramatically altered the manner in which this would normally be handled. Additionally, we had an exclusive. I chose to read the story unedited.

The fact the station claimed to be receiving complaint calls about the story didn't matter to me; there was hardly a day that went by that the station didn't get complaint calls. But a few months later, a letter arrived from the FCC. It stated that they had received a letter from a woman in Ballwin who said she was offended by what I'd read on the air, and that KSD was now facing a possible indecency fine.

Again, the system seemed backward to me. Instead of putting the focus on the crooked televangelists, the government seemed more interested in cracking the local radio guys for reading a story about it.

The entire industry was changing. Howard Stern's radio show was about to go into syndication around the country. Dozens of no-talent "shock jocks" were popping up all over the country and making things worse for everybody. And, while more and more radio stations were pushing the envelope with regard to "objectionable" material, television had discovered "trash talk" and "tabloid TV." Geraldo Rivera's infamous chair-throwing incident made the cover of *Time* magazine. Suddenly, controversy in the world of electronic media was all the rage.

For a time during the early and mid-eighties, the nationally syndicated *Sally Jessy Raphael* show emanated from the KSDK-TV studios in St. Louis. So when Executive Producer Burt DuBrow called from the show's new home in New Haven, Connecticut, asking me to appear on the show, I wasn't too surprised. Burt told me they were doing a show about music censorship and knew I was dead-set against it. The plan, he said, was to put me onstage next to the Peters brothers, a pair of evangelical ministers from Minneapolis who traveled from town to town, encouraging misguided youths to throw their Prince and Madonna albums on a huge bonfire after their evangelical "service." The two would take up a collection, then begin all over again in the next town.

I flew to New Haven after our show one morning in September of 1988. After an overnight stay in a musty hotel, I arrived at the television studio for the show's taping. The producers told me I'd be added to the panel about twenty minutes into the hour-long show, so I took a seat in front of a row of monitors in the green room. As the show began, my teeth just about fell out when Sally announced the topic would be "Evils in Your Children's Bedroom."

One by one, a bizarre panel of about a half dozen was introduced and briefly quizzed about his or her particular claim. One woman represented a society of atheists and insisted the violent images depicted in the Bible could give small children nightmares. A middle-aged sociologist believed Cabbage Patch dolls should be removed from stores because ... well ... I'm not sure the guest ever said why, but he sure was upset about them.

A third of the way into the show, a production assistant ushered me onto the stage, where I was wired up and given a seat next to the Peters brothers. I've never been meek when it comes to countering the kind of crap as they had been spewing, and I had my game-face on as I sat down.

As the Peters brothers held up album after album, each with a description of objectionable content and a itemized list of the objectionable aspects of many of the artists' personal lives, they took particular note of one R & B act. The act, the Peters pair claimed, required the concert promoter to provide a "rainbow assortment of condoms backstage after every concert."

"At least they're using condoms!" I interjected.

We were off to the races. Clearly, the Peters boys were not expecting someone like me. Over the next forty minutes they insulted me, shook fingers in my face and, all in all, totally lost their collective cool. They looked like raving maniacs.

"I thought ministers were supposed to have a ministry," I argued. "Instead, you guys are on *Entertainment Tonight!* There's Joan Collins talking about her new dress and Pee-wee Herman talking about his new movie, and you guys are in the middle! What are you doing on *Entertainment Tonight?* In the meantime, Minneapolis and St. Paul are turning into Sodom and Gomorrah because you're here instead of there!" I concluded.

I ᴉe times during the forty-minute period, the audience showed its approval for my comments with applause.

Postscript: *Despite my repeated attempts to settle the matter, the producers of the* Sally Jessy Raphael *show never got around to reimbursing me for the $1,000 plane ticket to New Haven.*

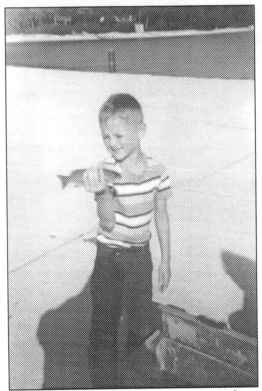

J.C. holds the 'catch of the day' during a family vacation in Door County, Wisconsin.

College days at Northern Illinois University In 1973.

Seated beside evangelical ministers, J.C. appeared on the *Sally Jessy Raphael* show to debate censorship.

"Partytown" drew a large crowd at the 1985 V. P. Fair alongside the *Admiral*. Where is J.C.?

In Dyersville, Iowa, J.C. stands in front of the house featured in the Kevin Costner film, *Field of Dreams*.

Pond scum? J.C. throws out the ceremonial first pitch prior to a Cards-Mets game at Busch Stadium.

On the left side of Highway 40/I-64, this billboard in 1985 proclaimed "The Morning Zoo" ...

On the right side, J.C. completed the coverage.

J.C. visits *Late Show* host David Letterman in '97.

At the first KSHE Comedy Show at Westport, (from left) Jerry Seinfeld, J.C., Larry "Bud" Melman, Paula Poundstone, and Wil Shriner posed together backstage.

J.C. with the KSD staff and Salvation Army officials at the 1989 "Food and Cash Salvation Bash."

Karen Kelly, Matuschka Lindo, Bob Costas, J.C., and Mike Bush smile for the camera at J.C.'s surprise 40th birthday party.

What's the frequency, J.C.?

Dad and J.C. stood on the roof of "Murphy's Bleachers" prior to the first night game at Wrigley Field in 1988.

"Music is like a pool. If you don't get a steady stream of fresh water in it, it starts to stink."

—Guitarist Pete Townshend

Chapter 20

By 1989 the show was hitting on all cylinders. Because KSD was a classic rock station, our promotion staff arranged for us to broadcast for a week from London as part of the twenty-fifth anniversary of The Beatles. The trip would include two shows from the historic Abbey Road Studios, where the band had recorded most of their music. The trip also was intended to test some of the new, satellite technology that had recently become available. (In fact, the transcontinental transmission back to St. Louis was so clear, the switchboard actually lit up with callers who refused to believe we were really in England!)

Sometimes it's better to be lucky than good. The day of our second broadcast, John Lennon's first wife, Cynthia, just happened to be in the building for the first time in sixteen years. Needless to say, we begged her to go on the air with us. She told stories of meeting John in art school and how driven he was as a performer. One of the "Apple Scruffs," immortalized in the song of the same name, talked about what it was like to be visited by the boys in the middle of the night on the steps leading into the building and how Paul frequently brought them food. But the tour of the building and the conversations with one of the Beatles' sound engineers who still worked there, were the highlights of the experience. Though Abbey Road was now a hi-tech, state-of-the-art recording facility, the studio where the band had done the bulk of its work with producer George Martin had purposely been left untouched, right down to the seaweed-stuffed drapery. Turns out it was the best available technology at the time to maximize the room's acoustics. We also saw the studio in which "Hey Jude" was recorded and, when I got back to St. Louis, I compared my photos and video to those in the documentary, *The Compleat Beatles.*

KSD's research indicated that the audiences really enjoyed hearing us do the show from remote locations, so we tried not to miss an opportunity. Of course, we were already broadcasting for a week from Cardinal spring training in St. Petersburg each year. When Bill Bidwill moved the football Cardinals to Arizona, we were right there on the day of their first game in a Monday night contest against the Dallas Cowboys. On St. Patrick's Day 1989, we did the show from the Hacienda Mexican Restaurant in West County. We took a group of eighty listeners and staff on a trip to Hawaii. We accompanied a busload of baseball fans to the actual *Field of Dreams* in Dyersville, Iowa, where the Kevin Costner movie was shot. For "Breakfast Club Across the Midwest," we rented an enormous Winnebago and did the show each morning from a different, small town in the region. We aired from Metropolis, Illinois, Home of "Superman"; Piedmont, Missouri, UFO Capital of the Midwest; Sedalia, Missouri, Home of the State Fair; Bado, Missouri, Population: Four; Sikeston, Missouri, Home of Throwed Rolls; New Madrid, Missouri, Earthquake Capital of Mid-America. The Winnebago experience was capped off by a Saturday afternoon show from a double-decker houseboat on the Lake of the Ozarks. The entire trip covered 1,500 miles.

And we started a nearly decade-long tradition in 1990 with our first week of live broadcasts from the Grammys in Hollywood. That week we presented live interviews with music stars such as Fleetwood Mac, Alice Cooper, Timothy Leary, Don Henley, Roger McGuinn and The Moody Blues, as well as show business, comedy, television and movie stars like Jerry Seinfeld, Steve Allen, David Hasselhoff, Richard Lewis, Super Dave Osborne, and more.

That trip also presented me with my first opportunity to attend the Grammys' telecast, to report from backstage, and to send a live report back to Channel Five via satellite. What a circus! The combination of the two-hour time change, the already ridiculous hours, and the TV/radio double duty meant there was little time for sleep. Yes, it was fun, but we were ***always*** working. As I remember it, that week in L.A. ranks as perhaps the best—and most exciting—of my entire radio career.

I say "as I remember it," because I spent the entire week on large doses of pain pills. I had gone on a press junket to Puerto Vallarta,

Mexico, to interview Kevin Costner (for the quickly forgotten movie *Revenge*) a few weeks earlier, and injured my back picking up a suitcase. I was finding it harder and harder to find a position in which to sit or to lie down that didn't cause me pain. While the rest of our crew was out on the town in L.A. enjoying Grammy week, I was spending the majority of free time in my room on my back.

I also spent the better part of one of those evenings on the phone with Jessica Hahn. Following our highly-publicized run-in with the FCC over the reading of her *Playboy* interview on the air, we finally had a chance to meet during the first-ever Arizona Cardinals football game in Phoenix. She had taken on a small role at a local radio station there, so we spent a few hours together just prior to her leaving for L.A. to shoot her part in the Sam Kinison video for *Wild Thing*. Now she was in L.A., one of the celebrities making the rounds and doing interviews during Grammy week.

It had been three years since her mega-scandal with Jim Bakker; her fifteen minutes had been up long ago. Her mother had just passed away, and Hahn was living alone in a Hollywood condo. Over the course of our two-hour-long conversation, I wondered how bad her life had to be if this woman, who was not much more than a casual acquaintance, apparently had only me to talk to. One minute she'd try to use slick, Hollywood jargon; the next minute, she'd sound like a lonely, confused little kid. After we hung up, I remember asking myself if I'd ever see her alive again.

(A year after that distressing phone conversation, she auditioned for a small role on the Fox sitcom, *Married with Children*. Not only did she get the part, she went on to marry the show's producer.)

We did take time out during the trip to see a taping of the *Tonight Show* via some tickets we squeezed out of Channel Five. Somehow we got shoved into the last row of the studio. Since it was a Monday, Jay Leno was the host and I had one of the NBC pages take him a note attached to my business card. During one of the commercial breaks, Jay had the audience in stitches when he started yelling things at me over the P.A. system like, "Hey, J.C.! Do you **know** somebody or something to be able to get such good seats?" After the show we met for a few minutes. I congratulated him on being named the permanent Monday night replacement for Johnny Carson. He thanked me for all the years of support.

Less than two weeks after I got back to St. Louis, I had to have major back surgery. A cervical disc had completely ruptured and had to be removed. The procedure involved a four-inch incision made in the *front* of the neck, the disc being removed and the fusion of a piece of bone from the "bone bank" where the disc had been. A gruesome, six-month recuperation required that I wear a large, hard, plastic neck brace nearly twenty-four hours a day. For the five minutes I was allowed to take it off each day to shower, it felt as though my head was simply going to roll off my shoulders and onto the floor. Though I wasn't allowed to drive for months, I returned to work just a week after being released from the hospital. For the first two weeks I was back, I had to walk to the program director's office and lie down on his couch for ten minutes every hour.

In January of 1990, KSD unveiled its plans for us to become St. Louis' first-ever radio show to perform a series of live broadcasts from Moscow in the former Soviet Union. This must have come as a horrible surprise to KMOX because forty-eight hours later they announced that *they* would be the first ever to broadcast from Moscow. The date we had given for the initial broadcast intended to commemorate Russia's annual May Day celebration—and to recognize the grand opening of the first McDonald's restaurant there—was Monday, April 30, 1990. The date KMOX gave for their first show was Friday, April 27. They were going to try to beat us by one day.

The local media flocked to the KMOX announcement while virtually ignoring us.

When we arrived in Moscow, I couldn't help but feel a chill upon seeing that hammer and sickle on the flag for the first time. We met up with our nineteen-year-old Russian guide and interpreter at the airport, where we were detained for two hours over a misunderstanding about the official reason for our visit. After we finally got clearance to pass through customs, we were taken by bus to the Intourist Hotel in the heart of downtown Moscow. Our accommodations could best be described as "primitive." Upon entering the bathroom, for example, we found towels the size and design of dishtowels and, yes, it *is* true what they say about Russian toilet paper. Of the rooms with televisions, few of them worked.

The people, on the other hand, were a hearty, friendly and curious group as we soon learned from the dozens of man-on-the-street interviews we conducted. A line of close to four hundred people snaked around the front of the McDonald's restaurant at lunchtime (where they would spend the equivalent of almost a month's worth of their salary for the privilege of sampling this American delicacy). We were astounded to learn there were thirty-nine cash registers inside the massive building. But the Big Mac I had that day proved to be the best meal I would have all week.

We heard The Beatles almost everywhere we went. The Muscovites seemed to know a surprising amount about the western world, particularly in the areas of pop culture and politics. But when questioned about American sports figures, they didn't hesitate to educate us on how badly Chuck Norris would be beaten if he fought in Russia!

I felt a sense of betrayal by my government early into the trip. After all, I had grown up during the Cold War and shared the belief held by many that the Russians were evil; a notion our government had taken pains to pound into us. But the Russians, as a people, seemed almost identical to us. It didn't take long to figure out that everything we'd been taught to believe was in reality a case of the Kremlin vs. the Pentagon.

Regardless of the revisionist history spewed forth by KMOX and cronies, the competing broadcasts in Russia did in fact result in two very different interpretations of this momentous accomplishment:

One broadcast featured a technically-challenged series of live segments moderated by Bob Hardy, transmitted via telephone quality line, consisting of Russian governmental representatives delivering long, dull, difficult-to-understand speeches, followed by a return to local programming until the next segment was ready. This version allows that KMOX should get credit for having the first-ever show originating from Moscow.

However, another group took its whole show and broadcast an entire, four-hour program via satellite. It was "J.C. and The Breakfast Club" on KSD; the first-ever show originating from Moscow.

"When it's said and done they haven't told you a thing."
—Singer/songwriter Don Henley

Chapter 21

I n this world there are only two kinds of people. Unfortunately, it seems as though too many of the wrong kind gravi-
tate to the world of media.

I've often said that television hates newspapers and newspapers
hate television ... but both hate radio.

Bias, questionable ethics and, in some cases, downright lying are
rampant in press coverage of the radio business. Case in point: If the
station engages in a charitable event or promotional effort, the news
departments' identify it as a "local radio station." Conversely, if a
radio personality of a station gets into trouble, say with the law, the
station's name is almost *always* used.

Not, I might add, that the radio industry has done much to put its
best foot forward over the last twenty years, either. The Motion Picture Association of America wisely throws its president, Jack Valenti,
in front of the news cameras and onto CNN's *Larry King Show* whenever there's a controversy threatening to portray the movie industry
in a negative light. Radio, on the other hand, has nobody to defend it,
even in those rare cases when a defense is justifiable.

A personal case in point:

In January of 1991, St. Louis Blues player, Paul Cavallini, suffered a
freak injury when Doug Wilson of the Chicago Blackhawks fired a
slapshot that cut off the tip of one of Cavallini's fingers. I thought I
was being clearly satiric about the rabid nature of diehard hockey
fans when I surmised, on the air, that Cavallini's finger was probably
in a jar in the hospital's pathology lab and we could probably raise a

lot of money for charity if we auctioned the finger off.

A few minutes later, a call came through from a female clerk at the hospital who whispered, "I have the finger."

Doubting the validity of the claim, I asked her for a phone number at the hospital where I could call her back. Sure enough, the number checked out and I found myself in what could only be described as morning show heaven. After getting a few laughs out of the situation, we moved on, explaining that Cavallini was expected to fully recover.

End of story? Not quite. In the January 6, 1991, edition of the *Minneapolis Star Tribune*, a reporter named Rachel Blount wrote a story, accompanied by the headline: "Sickies Make Light of Cavallini Injury." In the article, Blount said that "...the clerk was fired and the deejay was reprimanded and forced to apologize." Not only was the article completely untrue, no one at the station was even *aware* of the story until a listener, traveling through the Twin Cities, mailed the clipping to me. As if the situation could get any worse, the story was picked up nationally by the *Hockey News*, which meant it was being read throughout the entire North American continent. And it was all made up!

Often, when a small or niche paper has run a story critical of me, friends and colleagues haven't understood why I've cared. "Who's gonna see it?" they've often asked. But with the way stories are cannibalized and with no verification process in place, you tend to get a little paranoid.

And then there is the alternative press. In St. Louis, the *Riverfront Times*.

On the surface, a journalistic vehicle designed to go after stories too hot for the established, everyday paper to touch is a noble effort. Particularly in a one-newspaper town like St. Louis, somebody has to be there to talk about issues, stories and opinions that the *Post-Dispatch* can't get to, even when it's only due to the constraints of space. Every major city has its own version of the *Riverfront Times*. But I can only hope that the writers and editorial directors at the alternative papers in other cities speak to a higher ideal than what I saw from the *RFT* in the last decade.

As I see it, they were responsible for the darkest chapter of my professional career.

My relationship with the *Riverfront Times* had been uneven up until 1989. Though my political views leaned closer to the extremely liberal editorial position on which the publication was based, I thought a good portion of their act was pompous, overblown and just plain silly, and I often said so on the air. I felt they acted as if they were the self-appointed iconoclasts of the region and, if my guess is correct, didn't much care for the fact that J.C. Corcoran was finishing at the top of their own annual reader's poll in the category of "Best Radical," not to mention "Best Radio Show," "Best Radio Personality," and "Most Colorful Character."

I had also noticed that certain *RFT* columnists seemed to enjoy kicking people when they were down. During the six months I was off the air between jobs at KSHE and KSD, *RFT* music critic Terry Perkins took a swipe at me; in response, I sent a "Letter to the Editor" correcting two, factual errors in his story. A few days later I received a letter at my home, in which Perkins wrote:

"Your lame criticism doesn't really deserve a reply, but I thought you needed to know you are incapable of intimidating anyone. Hey, you can't even grow a decent beard. And here's another personal opinion for you. I think that short, prematurely-balding guys have strong tendencies to express their inadequacies through their belligerent attitude toward others. Look in the mirror and check it out."

Needless to say, for some reason, the people at the *RFT really* did not like me.

Nonetheless, though we fired shots back and forth occasionally, we peacefully co-existed for the most part. In fact, then-publisher Ray Hartmann had been a frequent guest on the show ever since I'd recognized him in the lobby of the Cardinals hotel during our live broadcasts from the 1987 World Series from Minneapolis and invited him onto our program. Ray also accompanied our broadcast team during the week of shows we did from Russia. We had, through these meetings, developed a decent, working relationship.

I'd been working with a brilliant KSDK videotape editor who was married to the principal photographer for the *RFT*. One day she began telling me about the *RFT*'s new media critic, a kid in his very early twenties by the name of Richard Byrne. According to her, Byrne had made it abundantly clear around the office that "J.C. Corcoran isn't going to be able to ignore me."

What did he mean by *that?* I wondered.

Before I had time to wonder just exactly what *that* meant, Byrne's pieces began to appear: bizarre, "left-field" criticism of local radio and television personalities, making it painfully obvious that he'd never spent a day in a television newsroom or around a radio station. One column ridiculed other reporters and me for showing too many cutaways during our one-on-one interviews with celebrities. Evidently, Byrne was unaware that he was taking exception to a basic television production tenet, in which edits are made from one point in the conversation to another in order to avoid what would appear as a "jump cut" in the video image on your screen at home. The edits are "covered' by a quick reaction shot to the reporter; a technique as elemental to television production as a baseball pitcher going to the resin bag. I remember thinking that if Byrne didn't know *that*, what else didn't he know?

The answer to that question came quickly. Week after week Byrne targeted the local media with column after column that more resembled prodding than criticism, and seemed to be more a reflection of his own, personal, narrow taste. In terms of our show, he complained that we didn't play enough music, while in the next breath ridiculed the kind of music we did play. He and cohort, Thomas Crone, repeatedly pounded us for not playing music by local bands. We tried to explain that KSD was a classic rock station and that we were, essentially, a talk show, but to no avail.

After almost two years of reading this nonsense, I picked up the *RFT* one day to find myself taken to task by then-columnist Thomas Crone over what he claimed was my ignorance of the local band, Uncle Tupelo. Though it was a cheap shot clearly designed to make me appear un-hip, I noticed there was a new photo of him. My partner, Joe "Mama Mason" and I noted that, as awful as this new photo was, anything was an improvement over Crone's last photo. "That one made him look like a big fag," I said.

The repercussions from those nine words *continue* to reverberate. But the immediate consequence, specifically over the course of the next five months, was far more devastating. I was labeled a "gay basher," and a smear campaign against me, instigated by a handful of people at the *RFT*, quickly took hold.

But first some personal philosophy.

I've always believed there's humor to be found in almost every topic or aspect of life, a belief that does not sit well with everyone. I enjoy talking openly about the things everybody insists should not be talked about. I can find humor, or rather irony, in almost everything, including death.

Particularly at the dawn of the politically correct era, my open discussion of things like the women's movement, the pro-life issue and homosexuality, and my efforts to find the funny parts of these topics, angered some, particularly the active, militant or self-appointed guardians of those issues. Some, especially the ones with a chip on their shoulder or the ones who didn't pay attention (and, by the way, they're often one and the same), argued that I was a bigot. Their message was clear: Talk about these sensitive areas in a less-than-reverent tone and we'll make your life miserable. Of course, this attitude merely resulted in my desire to discuss such "taboo" subjects even more.

Truth be known, I'd been a moderate Democrat most of my life. I've always been pro-choice, in favor of equal pay for equal work, as racially colorblind as possible and with very relaxed views about gays. Where I've parted with most minority groups is when their demand for "equal" treatment really means a demand for "special" treatment. And, while the point can be legitimately argued, I've always felt that jokes can be made about any minority issue—as long as the jokes aren't creepy, mean-spirited or malevolent in nature, and as long as a particular group isn't being disproportionately singled out.

In other words, at least socially, I'd always been quite liberal; a fact I thought I had made clear both publicly and privately.

Using that isolated comment in which I characterized Crone's picture as making him look like a "big fag," Crone, and particularly Richard Byrne, rallied the more excitable members of St. Louis' gay community in a frenzied and fanatical effort clearly designed to run me out of town on a rail. Nearly every week for the next five months the *RFT* printed columns, editorials, letters and other material, one more vicious and irresponsible than the next, accusing me of gay bashing, intended to further ignite public outcry. It wasn't unusual for a photo of me with my mouth open or a dumb look on my face to accompany the piece.

The *Post-Dispatch's* new media critic, Darrell McWhorter was next to jump aboard. Although I thought he was clueless and incompetent, this knowledge provided little consolation. Now the poison had made it outside the small, alternative paper universe and into the mainstream press. Some of my gay friends and acquaintances were beginning to ask questions. Others were feeling pressure because of their known relationships with me.

By now, the *St. Louis Journalism Review*, a very small, amateurish-looking publication was also blasting me. Their staff consisted mostly of former media employees, and there was no love lost between many of its staff writers and me. In the *SJR*, any story or column is accompanied by a "by-line." However, the stories about *me* were appearing without the by-lines, and I was unable to determine who was responsible for the vindictive attacks.

Byrne continued to ride the issue ferociously, attributing any minor fluctuation in KSD's ratings to the negative publicity. But the more we ignored him on the air, the more antagonistic Byrne became. Throughout our 1991 broadcasts from Grammy Week in New York, in our usual self-deprecating style, we complained about not being able to get good seats for the show or invitations into any of the good parties. (In all honesty, we were very well provided for, having even attended some private network and record company parties. But it was our habit, as we rubbed elbows with celebrities all week, to take ourselves down a notch so that our audience wouldn't think we were getting too big for our boxers.)

After our return, Byrne had the following to say about us in his March 6, 1991, column:

"Let me clue you in, fellas. You can't get good seats at the Grammys and entry into the good clubs because you're nerdy DJs from the Midwest. If you can't swallow the Big Apple, don't bite in it in the first place."

Still, we remained silent.

Finally, on March 20, 1991, a public meeting was held to confront KSD's management about the controversy. On one side of the table sat members of the St. Louis Effort for AIDS, Blacks Assisting Blacks Against AIDS, the AIDS Foundation of St. Louis, the Madison County AIDS Program, the St. Louis University HIV Vaccine Unit, Parents and Friends of Lesbians and Gays (P-FLAG), and Act Up.

On the other side sat KSD General Manager Merrell Hansen, KSD Program Director John Larson, and KSD Marketing Director Scott Strong.

For hours, the station's three managers were forced to listen to the ravings of a hysterical, screaming panel, one of whom accused me of being a "bigot," and "the Archie Bunker of the nineties."

Merrell Hansen, who'd had her fill of being pushed around by everyone from the VP Fair Committee to the Black Media Coalition, held her ground. In the summer of 1991, after nearly six months of harassment, Hansen and Ray Hartmann met for breakfast in West

County. When Merrell returned she told me there would be no more articles in the *Riverfront Times*. I wasn't given the details.

My anger hasn't subsided much over time. It was incredibly damaging to me both professionally and personally, and to this day I have to deal with the fallout. A wealth of hidden meanings was twisted into those nine little words, and I paid a substantial price for them.

But the most disturbing aspect of the entire controversy was that not one single person confronted the question: "Was J.C. Corcoran a bigot?" Regardless of whether my words could have been chosen more carefully when dealing with sensitive issues, gay or otherwise, I think that before someone is labeled with such negative connotations, such far-reaching implications and with such career-ending potential, there must proof-positive that the charge is correct. Although there are homophobes and gay-haters everywhere, I wasn't then, nor am I now, a bigot. The people at the *RFT* knew I wasn't a bigot. But they wrote that I was. Many on the staff at the *Post-Dispatch* knew I wasn't a bigot. But they let the stories run.

Postscript: Post-Dispatch *media columnist, Darrell McWhorter, died a short time later due to complications from AIDS.*

"My experience is that what makes a person grow is crisis."

—Actress Jane Fonda

Chapter 22

I'll never forget that 1991 Grammy week in New York. Only weeks before, the world had watched as the war in the Persian Gulf exploded in the skies over Iraq and, while virtually all the fighting had taken place in the air and via missile, fear was building that a much more gruesome ground war was unavoidable.

My wife Laura had introduced me to Emmett Kelly, a friend of hers who worked at NBC as the assistant to Tom Brokaw on the evening news. During a visit to the set, Emmett invited us to the dress rehearsal for that week's performance of *Saturday Night Live*. The "dress" is staged at exactly eight o'clock in front of a live audience and can, on occasion, be much more interesting to watch than the actual show. For one thing, as much as a half hour of extra material gets put on, with only the best ninety minutes making it to air at 11:30. Also, the sequence of sketches is often juxtaposed.

As we stood in a short VIP line for admittance to the studio, the sound of hurried footsteps began echoing from down the hallway. As the sound got closer, a frantic-looking young man in an NBC "page" uniform appeared from around the corner. Still running at full speed, the page made a bee-line for Emmett. The two huddled briefly in the corner. Emmett then took me aside, explaining that he wouldn't be able to attend the show with us because Brokaw had sent for him. "The ground war breaks out in two hours," Emmett informed me.

As I watched the rehearsal, I couldn't help but realize the United States was about to go to war and that many across the nation, as well as around the world, did not even know it yet.

The *SNL* show was supposed to open with Dana Carvey as George Bush dismissing his Cabinet from a meeting in the Oval office, only to walk into the next office to make a copy of a document where he would encounter "Richard," the famous "making copies" guy. But when the show aired three and a-half hours later, an announcement of the impending war was given, and Carvey's sketch was removed from the lineup.

As part of our special treatment that night, we were able to meet up with our friend, Emmett, at the *SNL* cast party around 2 a.m., at a restaurant on Manhattan's Upper West Side. Even though he had sat for a two-hour, in-studio interview with me just a few months before, Dana Carvey couldn't remember my name. But his first words to me were, "You're my favorite radio personality!" Later, Dana introduced me to Mike Myers, who upon learning I was from St. Louis, gushed with praise for Brett Hull. Myers even asked if I was in a position to arrange a meeting with the Blues' star! He also mumbled something about trying to finish a script for a movie that was based on his *SNL* character, "Wayne Campbell," of *Wayne's World.* Marci Klein, daughter of Calvin Klein, was draped over Phil Hartman at a table near a corner. And a wildly hyper Chris Farley was holding court in the center of the place while attempting to ride pony-back on the show's legendary producer, Lorne Michaels. My partner, Joe Mason, left the party around 4 a.m, with the host of a popular VH-1 program.

It had been quite a night. And I recall having a laugh over the ridiculous accusations from the *Riverfront Times* that we were somehow being overwhelmed and eaten up by the Big Apple.

If it's true something can get so big that it collapses under its own weight, maybe that's the simplest explanation for what happened in the months after we returned from that trip.

"J.C. and The Breakfast Club" was pulling outstanding ratings. Our sales staff was making money hand-over-fist. The top stars of the day were featured regularly. We executed dozens of fun, exciting promotions and events.

One memorable opening day broadcast at Ozzie Smith's sports bar and restaurant, we offered tickets to a guy if he could produce anything that was Cardinal red on him. After riffling through his pockets and wallet (even pulling out the elastic band of his underwear) failed to produce anything, he resorted to scratching off a scab!

We gave him the tickets.

But there was trouble in paradise.

From the time I met Joe "Mama Mason," I thought he was, well, "different." Joe wore his hair spiked on top and long in the back and his wardrobe was, well, odd. Joe, I thought, fashioned himself as a sort of Renaissance man. He was into psychology, science, foreign language and exotic travel. He also had a reputation as quite the ladies' man; quite a change from his teen years, when he was considered something of a nerd.

But professionally, I judged Joe on two criteria: his contributions to the show and his loyalty.

I liked the fact that Joe's head was always in the game and he usually had a good line to deliver, regardless of the occasion. He did enough work on the side to take some of the workload off me, and research indicated the audience really got a kick out of him.

As to Joe's loyalty, anyone who knows me knows I put a lot of stock in the concept of loyalty. You *have* to be able to trust your on-air partner. There is an obscene amount of backstabbing and overall b.s. in this business and it just requires too much energy to constantly look over your shoulder and see who's operating against you. So on that second criteria, Joe passed with flying colors. Joe and I were on the same page with regard to how the show should be done; a mutual commitment that was worth its weight in gold to me. And when anyone started in with rumors or accusations about Joe, I'd immediately make it clear I would entertain none of it. Joe, Don "D.J." Johnson and I were a team; we needed to be able to count on one another.

This very issue of loyalty moved to the forefront in the late eighties when Dan Caesar, the sports media columnist for the *Post-Dispatch*, caught our co-host, Don "D.J." Johnson, in the press box at Busch Stadium on what was apparently a bad night. D.J.'s contract was up and Joe's lawyer (who had also taken on D.J. in an attempt to negotiate a new deal with KSD) was filling his head with lots of counterproductive nonsense. According to a subsequent Caesar column, D.J. had claimed that, on road trips, he was doing all the work for the show while Joe and I got to go to "all the parties." This, of course, was ridiculous. But it couldn't have been more obvious that the article was intended to embarrass us, given the fact that Caesar never even bothered to pick up the phone to get a comment from Joe or me.

Contract negotiations, particularly when they're not going well, can be a nightmare, and I didn't hold anything against D.J. for his poorly chosen words. I'm sure he was just blowing off steam and never imagined Caesar was going to print his comments. But things were never the same for D.J. after that incident. After several failed attempts to get his own sports show on the air, his contract wasn't renewed and he left KSD.

From its humble beginning four years before, our annual Christmas fundraiser to benefit the Salvation Army had grown into an enormous civic event. It now required six months to adequately stage the production. The tireless efforts of Cathy Kelly and Scott Strong in our marketing and promotion department; producers Judy Martin and Libby Kochan; production director, Everett Marshall; Dave Obergoenner, Scott Clifton, Bruce Cavins and "B.R."—a very sweet, older man with a strong resemblance to "Uncle Fester" from the *Munsters*, who actually agreed to pose for a picture with a light bulb in his mouth!—from the engineering department; plus countless individuals at the original location of West County Center and later Chesterfield Mall; the Salvation Army; KSDK; and dozens of other businesses and organizations produced, perhaps, the most amazing results in St. Louis radio promotion history. The thirty-hour live broadcast of the 1990 "Food and Cash Salvation Bash" raised almost $70,000, as well as over twenty tons of food for needy families.

Because the event had grown to such magnitude, I agreed to turn over control of the live musical portion of it to Joe and his friends and acquaintances in the local music business. While the rest of us worked on booking appearances by almost every major television personality in town to sing as part of "The Brain Damaged Media Dorks," Joe secured the musicians to play in the enormous band.

While all this was going on, I was in a fight with KSD's management and, in particular, the sales department over another issue. Without my knowledge, the station was distributing "Food and Cash Salvation Bash" sales kits to its account executives. Their intent was to incorporate the event and make money for the station off the "Bash." By taking what had always been considered a "pure," charity event and charging higher rates for commercial time during its thirty hours, management was turning it into a money-making sales promotion. I vehemently argued that the plan completely violated the spirit of the event, and made it abundantly clear what I thought of their decision to do it behind my back. The sales staff appeared dumbfounded by my reaction, and proceeded with their plan in spite of my objections.

Although the 1990 "Bash" proved a tremendous success, a few weeks later I learned there had been lots of things going on backstage that would have caused great embarrassment to the Salvation Army and the station. The innocence of this Christmastime event had been seriously compromised and I was seriously angry with the individuals I felt were responsible.

With the beginning of the new year my relationship with Joe continued to show signs of strain. On more than one occasion we had reason to question the accuracy of his statements, the validity of his claims and, in at least one case, his "location." It had always been our habit to call into the show, even during time off. And after one of Joe's regular trips to Europe, we learned the calls he said he'd been making from France had actually been made from Denmark. I dismissed the incident, figuring he must have had his reasons.

I'd been married for less than six months, and had begun to notice Joe acting differently toward me. He appeared distant, evasive. Even others at the station were beginning to talk, saying the stories he had told them-concerning fairly inconsequential matters-weren't matching up.

The station had been co-sponsoring a series of happy hours and other events with Carlsberg Beer, a subsidiary of Anheuser-Busch, and had flown a recent winner of the Miss Denmark Pageant, Pia Larsen, to St. Louis to help out. It wasn't long before Joe and Pia were dating and, a year or so later, announced their engagement. It wasn't until a few months later that Joe got around to telling me that Pia had suddenly returned to Denmark, and the engagement was off. I found the whole episode strange, especially Joe's reticence to discuss the reasons for the breakup. Our off-the-air relationship was beginning to unravel.

As if this whole sideshow with Joe wasn't enough trouble, there were growing indications from Gannett Broadcasting's corporate boys in L.A. that we were more unpopular with them than ever. KSD was the bastard child of their group of radio stations. We were the only classic rock—or *any* kind of rock—station in the company. We didn't seem to fit the company mold, and the suits weren't shy about letting us know it. This impression, of course, irked us to no end, since we were responsible for one of the most productive cash cows in their group. They thought we were jerks and we felt the same way about them. We'd also made a huge stink over the fact that Gannett's crown jewel, *USA Today*, regularly went to KMOX instead of us—their own flesh and blood—with an annual Major League Baseball All-Star game balloting contest. And, finally, there was that little issue of my salary, which had now grown to an annual mid-six-figure base, before bonuses.

Though I'd had a generally good relationship with KSD's general manager, Merrell Hansen, we were now arguing a great deal, much of the time about the deteriorating situation involving Joe. What followed was a period of months without speaking to each other at all.

In the summer of 1991, while juggling the worsening situation with Joe and the growing feeling of hostility emanating from Gannett corporate, I successfully engineered a deal for the station to give away an in-ground swimming pool. In July the pool was installed at the winner's home in St. Charles and, as part of the promotion, we did the show live from the listener's back yard. Half the neighborhood was in and out of the pool and in and out of the house, all morning long. There was a terrific, upbeat, party atmosphere throughout the show.

Three days later, near the end of the show, Karen Kelly, a young, enthusiastic intern who had recently come aboard, took me aside. She told me she'd been out in the office and hallways, and sensed something big was coming down. Indeed, the second the show was over, Merrell grabbed Joe for a closed-door meeting. I was alone in a production studio when Merrell and Program Director John Larson came in. Their expressions were grim.

"Sometimes when someone is really mad about something their anger can be displayed in very unusual ways," Merrell said. "Is there anything you'd like to tell us?"

Not having the slightest idea what she was talking about (but sensing something ridiculous was coming), I asked her to get to the point.

Have you ever had the feeling that you are having an out-of-body experience?

Merrell said she'd received an angry complaint from the winners of the swimming pool contest: someone had defecated in their bathtub sometime during our show.

I was stunned by the revelation. I was even more astonished when I realized that the two seemed to suspect me!

Anger, resentment, even rage emerged as the discussion went on for nearly an hour. And although neither Merrell nor John would admit it, I suspected that Joe had had a hand in placing the blame on me. I spent the next few days completely at a loss. After having worked so long with these people and in such an intimate environment, how could they even *think* I was responsible for such a vile and pathological act? I wondered.

My relationship with Joe had suffered a series of irreparable blows. The trust and loyalty I'd been so insistent upon when we began as a team was gone.

I called upon the assistance of a licensed therapist to make some suggestions as how to best handle this increasingly volatile situation. My subsequent, private meetings with Joe hit an early dead end.

One morning I was called to the lobby. Joe's father was waiting for me, holding a fairly large box in his hands. In it was an expensive, ceramic pitcher. When I asked why he had given me such a gift, he responded, "I just want to thank you for everything you've done for my boy." Then he turned and walked out.

On September 25, 1991, I got a call around 8:30 p.m. from my special projects producer, Judy Martin, who was still at the station. She told me Merrell and Joe had been in a meeting in Merrell's office for several hours. Judy and I spoke for a while about how incredibly odd that was.

Immediately following the show the next morning, I raced to Merrell's office. But instead of learning what had transpired the night before, I was met with a decidedly cold and impersonal reception. Whatever had happened last night, the fact was that Merrell was now against me, too.

Speechless, I walked back to the office I shared with Joe, closed the door and met with my partner for the last time. This time, though, he went on the offensive. Things got ugly fast. I stood and pleaded with him to simply talk to someone about what was going on, leaning toward him over my office chair. When he bristled at the suggestion and made a crack about having Merrell on his side, I shoved the chair into the corner of the office, where it fell on its side. I opened the door only to find Merrell standing directly in front of it. I swept past her, stepped outside, and began walking the streets of the Corporate Square building complex.

I felt as though I didn't have any options.

I couldn't just go on the air the next day as though nothing happened. And now I had no idea what Merrell believed.

When I finally returned to the building, Merrell met me at my office door. I told her I felt she had a situation on her hands that had spun out of control. I said that I was taking a leave of absence and that she should call me when she felt the situation was under control again. I gathered some things, drove home, and called my lawyer.

Close to ten o'clock that night, Jeff called to say he was returning to his office in Clayton. He was going at the request of Gannett's corporate attorneys in order to receive a fax. He called a half-hour later to tell me that the station would honor the remaining seven months on my contract, but that I would no longer be working at KSD.

To say I was shocked by the news would be an understatement.

Somehow, my efforts to help my friend and partner, a move that had been supported, even encouraged, by management had blown up in my face. I was the one who was now without a job. But my refusal to play Gannett's stupid political games, coupled with the corporate guys' long-standing resentment toward us, probably figured into the equation, too. I'd been working without a net for far too long.

Joe immediately seized the opportunity and became the interim host of the show, but not before allegedly spreading the rumor that I'd thrown a chair at him during our final meeting. And, when you think about it, it was a brilliant maneuver on his part. Everyone already thought I was a maniac, so why not completely misdirect everyone with a story that deflected all the attention away from him? Within a few days, the story had expanded to my having thrown a chair at Merrell.

The station issued a short, vague explanation for my dismissal, stating "a decision was made that J.C. would no longer work at KSD," carefully avoiding the word "fired." But the local media still had a field day with the story. Having no real information to go by, some members of the media told the story the way they **hoped** it had happened, complete with ridicule, snickers and suppositions.

The following week, the newly appointed news director at KSDK (a man referred to not-so-affectionately as "Kermit," because of his resemblance to the famous frog) eliminated the station's entertainment budget. After six years of service with Channel Five, my job there was taken away, too. I've always believed the two incidents were related.

A few weeks later, the summer Arbitron ratings were released. "J.C. and The Breakfast Club" had achieved the highest numbers in six years, out-distancing both KSHE **and** KMOX with first-place finishes in both the 25- to 49-year-old-adult listeners and the 18- to 34-year-old male categories. It also meant KSD, according to the terms of my contract, had to write me a $25,000 bonus check, in addition to the $248,000 in remaining salary.

KSD decided to go ahead with the 1991 "Food and Cash Salvation Bash," and although I held the legal copyright to the name, I chose not to challenge the station's use of it. My only involvement came in the final fifteen minutes of the event. Right from its beginning, I had made a pledge to myself to donate a thousand dollars for each year the "Bash" had been in existence. I'd had ankle surgery in October and was still on crutches, but I managed to make it to the mall in time to hand a check to the Salvation Army representative for $5,000. Then I turned and walked out. I never made eye contact with anyone from the station.

Over the course of the next year, along with a group of local investors, I amassed about $1.3 million as part of an attempt to purchase a local FM station. What was then known as KATZ-FM (100.3) was on the block, and our group worked hard and spent a ton of money preparing to buy it out of receivership. A few months before the deal was to go down, though, the FCC issued its historic ruling that changed the ownership rules for American radio properties. (Until this ruling took effect in 1992, a company was not allowed to own more than one AM and one FM station per market.) With the new ruling, the door was opened for multiple station ownership, which sent the prices for stations, even bad ones, skyrocketing. We were out of business before we had a chance to begin.

Back at KSD, it was determined early on that Joe "Mama Mason" wasn't going to succeed as the show's primary host. For a while, Mike Bush was brought in, followed by Kevin Slaten. Finally, after the morning show plummeted to seventh place, a reconciliation was attempted between KSD and me.

Cathy Kelly, Judy Martin, Eric Mink and others associated with the station, never gave up on the idea that the two sides might somehow get back together. I'm sure this belief was based largely on the fact that Merrell and I had been so close, and our relationship was more like brother and sister than an employer and employee. When I learned my wife, Laura, was pregnant in September of 1992, I thought this might be a good time to see if there was a chance at a reconciliation. Merrell and I met at Stacy Park in Olivette and, within minutes, our smiles were back.

Merrell and I decided that I would return to KSD's morning show as part of a simulcast with KSD-AM (550). At 9 a.m., the FM would split off to a mostly music format while we continued on the AM with talk, followed by Rush Limbaugh and other local and syndicated programming, which I would have a large part in overseeing. After months of planning and negotiating, the deal blew up unexpectedly. It wasn't until a few months later that I learned Gannett's long-rumored plan to get out of the radio business had finally come true. It seemed as though they couldn't wait to unload their St. Louis properties.

Postscripts: *One morning, the parent company of Y98 walked in and took KSD over. Inside the envelope each employee received was a slip of paper indicating whether you still had a job or not. Roughly half the building was let go. Frank O. Pinion was installed as new morning host.*

Joe "Mama Mason" quit.

We haven't spoken to each other since September 26, 1991.

"History depends on who writes it."
—President Richard Nixon

Chapter 23

The majority of the television work I'd been doing for Channel Five fell into the category of light entertainment. *Post-Dispatch* critic, Joe Pollack, did the movie "reviews" while I handled the celebrity interviews. Pollack made no secret of the fact he was irked by having to share the stage with "a disc jockey," and the two of us rarely spoke, on or off the set.

But KSDK and Pollack parted ways in 1990 and he popped up across town at KMOV. In a *St. Louis Journalism Review* column shortly after my untimely departure from Channel Five, staff writer Don Corrigan wrote that Pollack must have gotten a "fairly good belly laugh" upon hearing about my termination. I, in turn, got a fairly good belly laugh upon reading that column, since I knew both Pollack and another entertainment reporter, Dawn Meadows, were about to be replaced by me.

I'd had several conversations with Channel Four's management while I was still with Channel Five. I'd been bugged by the fact that I hadn't ever received a raise, and, despite having won an Emmy for my 1989 half-hour special entitled, "J.C. Went to Cardinal Spring Training and All We Got Was This Lousy TV Show," the station never let me do another one.

In July of 1992 I began what would turn out to be a seven-year-long stint as entertainment editor at KMOV, two floors immediately below the "Voice of St. Louis."

In the fall of 1992, following the death of Bob Hyland, CBS's newly installed general manager of KMOX, Rod Zimmerman, announced

Tom Langmyer as the station's new program director. I hadn't seen Tom since 1984, when he held down the overnight shift at the AM "sister station" of "97 Rock," the same outlet where I had been doing mornings in Buffalo. I dropped him a congratulatory note and, a few weeks later, we met for lunch across the street at the Adam's Mark Hotel. Near the end of the meal, he nonchalantly asked, "So, what would you think about coming over?"

"You mean, like, for dinner with you and Mary?" I asked.

As he proceeded to tell me how much he thought I could help the station, I recall a cracker getting stuck midway down my throat.

I told Tom I thought his idea was intriguing. But what I was really thinking was that my friend, an avid hockey player, appeared to be suffering the lingering effects of playing without his helmet.

It wasn't until January of 1993 that I ran into Tom again. I was on a plane to New York to interview the anchors of the *CBS Evening News*, *48 Hours*, and *60 Minutes* for a series on Channel Four, when I ended up being seated in the row ahead of Tom and Rod Zimmerman. Tom introduced me to Rod, and we all talked for a good portion of the flight. After many follow-up meetings, in which we discussed everything from direction to strategy to contractual matters, a news conference was called one, snowy day in February of 1993 with "a major programming announcement at KMOX."

For a year and a half, ever since my "suspicious" departure from KSD, I'd been the subject of dozens of articles, columns, industry gossip and downright character assassination by those claiming to know things that they really didn't. This outpouring was followed by the ridiculous speculation that I'd pissed off too many people, burned too many bridges, and that my career was over.

Imagine the perverse glee I took in walking out in front of the media, sitting down in front of the microphone, and announcing I'd be taking over the afternoon drive slot at K-M-O-freaking-X!

As fate would have it, the next day I happened to come face to face with the sixty-nine-year-old, longtime host of KMOX's mid-afternoon show, Anne Keefe, in the crowded restaurant adjacent to the station. Considering we were in full view of dozens of KMOX and KMOV staffers who were having lunch, I had no choice but to say **something**. Keefe angrily rebuffed my overtures, and word quickly spread of the awkward encounter.

Of course, Keefe was livid over Zimmerman's decision to hire someone she viewed as the anti-Christ and made no secret of her feelings on *Donnybrook*, the weekly, local public broadcasting television show on which she was a contributor.

In the month between the official announcement and my first day on the air, roughly eight hundred angry letters, countless phone calls and even a few "we-might-carry-more-weight-if-we-come-in-person" visitors to the station, descended upon the office of Rod Zimmerman. I read almost all of the letters and pointed out to Tom Langmyer how many seemed to have been written by the elderly. This fact was borne out by the crooked handwriting that angled up the side, the use of a greeting card instead of stationery, and signed with names like "Elmer," "Bittie," "Agnes," and other names that hadn't been assigned to children in over seventy years.

In an unprecedented move, Zimmerman twice got on the air in an attempt to calm the hysterical throngs. Obviously, he felt the pressure. Before I ever spent a single day on the air, I had been issued a long list of people, companies and topics I was instructed not to talk about. Additionally, the station quickly installed a new format into the 4- to 6-p.m. portion of my 3- to 6-p.m. timeslot, converting the longtime "talk" presentation into a rapid-fire "news and information" delivery. Now, instead of having ten- to fifteen-minute blocks of uninterrupted time to talk, take calls and develop topics, I now had four and a half minutes. Accounting for news, traffic, sports, weather, commercials and other material, my total time on mic per hour was roughly twelve minutes. The station also instituted a policy of broadcasting "traffic and weather together every ten minutes," though I often jokingly remarked that it felt more like every ten seconds.

At 3:10 p.m. on March 15, 1993, more than seventeen months after my last show at KSD, I hit the air on KMOX. My first words were, "Well, there goes the neighborhood." My first guest was Brett Hull of the St. Louis Blues, who graciously sat in with me for the entire first hour. Later in the show I got a call of support from Matt Hyland, son of the station's departed, inspirational leader. I heard later that his sister, the woman I'd made the joke about when she was the Veiled Prophet queen over eight years ago, called her brother to complain about his call.

As for the miniscule segment of the audience and press that had an open mind, the early reviews weren't bad.

But it was all over before it even began.

I had lost the battle over who would be my producer, having asked for Karen Kelly, my KSD intern who had shown great promise and having received, instead, a young man who'd been doing a series of odd jobs around the station. Zimmerman wanted him and, because I wanted to appear cooperative, I agreed. Within days, the new "producer" and I had problems. It became obvious he'd led a sheltered life and, thus, it became a chore to have to first educate him as to who Jack Valenti or Edwin Newman was before we could get into a discussion about booking them, and what sort of path the interview might take.

It was my intent to pick up the pace of the show by using musical themes as adjoiners or to introduce certain segments and interviews, but when the guy had to ask twice about the name of a Beatles' song, "...something with 'Jude' in the title?" I thought things were getting ridiculous. I had also been noticing that he would practically race out of the station each evening at six o'clock and head to the Adam's Mark Hotel across the street. He was a born-again Christian, so that ruled out "AJ's." When I finally asked him, he told me that "AJ's" had a free buffet during happy hour; he could eat free every night.

I'd finally had enough of this "cooperative" agreement, and insisted I be allowed to hire Karen as producer.

Karen and I were given cubicles on what we called "the-second-and-a-half" floor; a sort of *Being John Malkovich* scenario. Call it a glorified attic, complete with dark brown wood paneling, nicotine-stained ceiling tiles and suspicious-looking marks on the walls. We only guessed that the area didn't even show up on the building's blueprints. We were completely cut off from the rest of the radio station, except, of course, from the only other person who, on occasion, drifted in and out of the only remaining cubicle in our little space, a blind guy with Tourette's syndrome.

Let me repeat that statement.

We shared our cramped, dark, archaic, deserted office space with a blind guy with Tourette's syndrome.

From what we could gather, as part of CBS' massive, equal opportunity requirement, KMOX must have agreed to allow him to participate in the station's activities, though nobody seemed to have the foggiest idea as to what those activities might be. All Karen and I knew was that we'd be on the phone attempting to nail down an interview slot with Mike Wallace or Rev. Jesse Jackson, and we'd suddenly find ourselves in the unenviable position of having to explain why someone just yelled a string of obscenities in the background.

Anne Keefe continued to refuse to acknowledge my presence, either on the air or off. In reading the line-up of shows, interviews and features that were scheduled later in the day, she would systematically ignore my 3- to 6-p.m. shift. Each day at three o'clock, she'd walk out of the studio via one door and I'd walk in the other. People at the station argued whether the process was more like something you'd see on a submarine or in a zoo.

Over the course of those first few weeks, I deliberately hung around the station during the times other major KMOX personalities like Bob Hardy and Jim White were in the building. I wanted a chance to get to know them, and vice-versa. None of them would speak to me. In fact, when I specifically asked White if Anne Keefe had anything to do with the cold shoulders, he responded, "I'm not going to get caught in the middle of this."

I did know many of the KMOX sports guys and, in fact, had had several private conversations with Joe Buck over the years. I had always been irritated over the ongoing commentary by people who apparently thought they were handing Joe a compliment when they'd credit Joe's baseball play-by-play talent to being Jack's son; as if, somehow, the ability to call an exciting, three-hour game could be traced to genetics. I told Joe I knew it was good, old-fashioned hard work that made him such a successful broadcaster. Joe appreciated my remarks, and we've had a good relationship since.

Soon Anne Keefe announced her plans to retire from broadcasting effective in the fall. When asked directly in a KMOV interview by Laurie Waters if her announcement had anything to do with KMOX's hiring of J.C. Corcoran, Keefe said "no." But Keefe told everyone *else* in the world the exact opposite.

Karen and I tried to make the best of what we had to work with. In fact, we landed huge interviews with some of the biggest celebrities, journalists, sports figures and entertainers of the day. Fueled by extremely genuine words of support from KMOX fixtures like Ron Jacober, Bob Hamilton, news director John Angelides and others, we forged ahead. Several of the stalwart engineers, who'd been around since the station was built, insisted I was doing some of the most exciting and entertaining stuff they'd heard since the Jack Carney heydays. Bob Costas, whom I'd called for advice the night before the KMOX announcement was made, also made an in-studio appearance. One of our most surprising supporters was Wendy Wiese, whom I'd riddled with jokes and criticism years before when she was doing the morning show on KMOX. Our shots at her had stopped, though, when I learned of her first pregnancy. Though our schedules at the station rarely coincided, Wendy and I developed a friendship, which mystified the very few around the station who were even aware of it.

However, I could sense incredible restlessness within the station regarding my presence. There's a lot you can tell just by the way management greets you in the hallway. Outside the station I was being massacred by the old-guard; the hard-line, KMOX legion of fans, many of whom, I'm certain, believed Bob Hyland was still alive.

Frank Absher, a columnist for the *St. Louis Journalism Review* (more famous for phoning Bob Hyland to rat on KMOX on-air hosts whom Absher felt had given a substandard performance than anything else) allegedly proclaimed in public that I was being paid the paltry sum of forty grand a year. (For the record, Absher wasn't even in the neighborhood.)

It was policy that the station's seven-second delay unit was to be activated whenever the phone lines were opened to callers. The unit, however, was not activated during conversations with guests who were interviewed by phone. So we had no reason to believe an individual we'd booked one afternoon for an interview about college politics would present a problem. Early in the conversation, my eyes locked onto Karen's on the other side of the glass. We each thought our ears must have been playing tricks on us when we heard the "f" word. Our guest uttered the "f" word again. I immediately cut him off, apologized to the audience and went to a commercial.

The fact that it could have happened to anyone on the station didn't matter. You might as well have announced over the station's public address system, "Let the crucifixion begin!"

One afternoon I played a hilarious comedy routine by Tim Allen, in which he remarks that his nipples get hard when he walks through the tool section at Sears. Minutes later, Rod Zimmerman entered Karen's producer booth to ask if she had access to a mechanism with which she could cut me off the air.

It was a few days later that David Koresh's Branch Davidian complex went up in flames just outside Waco, Texas. Zimmerman informed me I was being replaced for that day by Nan Wyatt of KMOX's news department.

The following week I began private talks with Barry Baker, whose claim to fame had been converting Channel 30 from primarily a religious and block programming station into a Fox Network affiliate.

Baker had picked several weak-signaled radio stations along the way, and I'd heard he was in the process of upgrading one of those outlets. I explained that although I believed I was doing good work at KMOX, the atmosphere was completely unproductive, and that a move back to FM might benefit us both. Baker indicated he was still a few months away from completing his deal, but that an opportunity would probably present itself at that time.

It was about this time that the morning team of "Steve and D.C.," on a local, rinky-dink Top 40, committed what was, arguably, the worst blunder in St. Louis radio history. For several months the two had seemingly been playing a racist radio version of Russian roulette—featuring everything from trash-talking bigoted rednecks to the airing of actual Ku Klux Klan records. But one morning a young, black caller named Nicole Hammonds dared to take issue with their racist rant. Nineteen-year-old Isaiah Wilhelm, aka, D.C. Chymes, then screamed the epithet, "n*****," at her. "Now you're acting like an ignorant n*****," he repeated.

Steve & D.C. were pulled off the air and, subsequently, fired in an unprecedented firestorm of public outrage. A variety of civic, religious and private groups held news conference, denouncing what had taken place. But, in relating this despicable incident on KTVI's news, the reporter referred to the offending radio personality as "D.C. Corcoran."

Now *my* name had been mistakenly dragged into the story.

On that week's edition of *Donnybrook* on Channel Nine, the show opened with an obviously rehearsed, scathing diatribe by Anne Keefe during which, *not* Steve & D.C. *but* J.C. Corcoran, was her target. For over eleven minutes of prime television time Keefe unloaded an unbridled attack on my character, blaming me for, in essence, the fall of western civilization as we know it. She claimed she couldn't understand why this incident was getting so much attention when "Mr. Corcoran's sexist insults, which aired all throughout the 1980s, went almost unnoticed." She repeatedly spoke on behalf of Wendy Wiese, whom she continued to "defend," unaware of, or indifferent to, the fact that Wendy and I were pals. Clearly, Keefe saw an opportunity to drag me down to the level of what I considered two, poorly educated, white-trash racists.

During the shift change at three the next afternoon, I sarcastically thanked Keefe for her continuing, inspirational display of professionalism. The next thing I knew, longtime producer Fred Zielonko was trying to separate us. General Manager Rod Zimmerman and Program Director Tom Langmyer were waiting for me at six o'clock that evening, stern looks on their faces. I handed them a tape of Keefe's comments she had made on TV the night before, and headed back to my office. Presumably, they must have thought I'd gone home for the night because when I went back to get their reactions to the tape, I heard laughter coming from the office.

Not long after, a dim, new reporter for the *St. Louis Business Journal* named Howard Lerner called a few minutes before three one afternoon to ask a litany of questions about what was going on with KMOX and me. In my efforts to hurry him along and remain cooperative, I apparently did not choose my words carefully enough. A few days later the headline appeared, "Corcoran Chafes at KMOX: Changes too slow, airtime too little." In attempting to characterize my "affection" for Keefe, Lerner sandwiched the term "senile" in between a series of quotes from the interview, mistakenly creating the impression I had used the word to describe her.

Rod Zimmerman fired me the day the paper hit the newsstands.

The press had a field day, again cannibalizing one another's stories. The *Post-Dispatch* quoted the *Business Journal*. The television stations quoted papers, reporting I'd **called** Keefe "senile." Mike Owens at Channel Five reported, "Corcoran's stint at KMOX was marked by frequent scraps with fellow employees," which, of course, was completely untrue. (I got along well with everyone who spoke to me.) A letter-to-the-editor at the *Post* from Rebekah Donne of Kirkwood read:

> *"I stopped listening [to Corcoran] on KSD more than two* years ago after a woman called in and dared to disagree with Corcoran on some issue or other. He backed up slightly from the microphone, shouted "You whore!" and hung up on her, much to the amusement of his *co-disc jockey."*

Total fiction. The incident Donne claimed happened, never did.

A KMOV reporter named John Hall did a story for the ten o'clock news, which included commentary from an advertising executive I'd never even heard of, wearing a bad toupee and claiming to be an expert. There was also a stand-up by Hall in front of my desk in the Channel Four newsroom. "J.C. could often be heard complaining about his treatment at KMOX from his desk here at Channel Four,"

Hall sternly proclaimed.

It was one of the most blatant violations of professional trust I'd ever seen.

Most amusing of all, however, were Anne Keefe's comments to *the Post-Dispatch* in its Saturday, May 29, 1993, edition: "It's a shame, isn't it? Some people are self-destructive. I feel sorry that Mr. Corcoran apparently can't seem to get along with management, which is something we all have to learn to do."

Keefe had pulled off a textbook back-stab.

Postscripts:

My brief, three-month stint at KMOX wasn't a complete loss. I was able to confirm what I had always suspected: the station's program director, Robert Osborne, had, in the 1980s, regularly taped my shows at KSHE and KSD and sent excerpts to the FCC.

Addison Clark Corcoran, our first child, had been born three weeks earlier. I put together a series of soundbites on the air from films like Raising Arizona, She's Having a Baby *and* Prelude to a Kiss, *against a musical background of Stevie Wonder's "Isn't She Lovely," to welcome her into the world.*

John Hall moved to Boston later that year.

Anne Keefe, amidst accolades, retired in the fall.

Someone told me Howard Lerner left The St. Louis Business Journal *about a year later to open a coffee shop.*

"Happiness and success are not the same thing."
–Singer/songwriter "Sting"

Chapter 24

I began the morning show at Barry Baker's station in August of 1993. The "Fox," (101.1 FM) as it was known, suffered from weak programming, a weak on-air staff and an equally weak signal. I took the job with the understanding the broadcast tower would be moved closer to downtown St. Louis within six months; a move that would allow the station to be competitive with the other St. Louis FMs.

Ken Anthony, the new program director from Los Angeles had just made The Fox's sister station, "The Point," into a huge success, and was now being given the reins of our station, too. He was the quint-essential radio "dude," who wore ten-year-old velour clothes from Chess King, complete with the top two or three buttons of his shirt open. We understood he had a wife and children back in California.

I'd worked with Matuschka Lindo at Channel Five a few years before, but she'd since left television and married KSDK sports re-porter, Malcolm Briggs. When she expressed interest in the co-host-ing and news-reading duties, I quickly offered her the job. And Karen Kelly just about laid rubber in the KMOX parking garage, ecstatic about getting out of there and rejoining me as producer.

It became clear, very early on, that there was a reason this station had never been a ratings winner. The entire facility seemed to be in a constant state of chaos. The "Fox" was located in the Channel 30 building at Cole and Tucker, at the north end of downtown. Hardly a month went by when we didn't hear about some sort of violent crime somewhere within a few hundred feet of us. One of our female account executives gassed up her car at the service station across the street one Friday afternoon and when she returned from paying at the booth, the car was gone. (They found it in Colorado or Utah or somewhere a few days later.) Another time, as our program director walked the block and a half to the satellite lot reserved for station personnel one evening, he noticed the dome light in his car was on. As he got closer, he could see two legs protruding from the open door. When he screamed at the top of his lungs, the thief who was attempting to hot-wire the vehicle scampered off. Charles, the sometimes-overzealous, Channel 30 security guard, arrived on the scene a few seconds later complaining, "Why did you yell? I could have shot him!"

Only a few weeks after I started, the general manager was replaced by one of the *screwiest* people I've ever met. The program director, Ken Anthony, was almost completely immersed in the activities at the Point, and so, turned over the majority of control of The Fox to Suzanne Michaels, the mid-day woman. Given her lack of qualifications for this position, many of us suspected something more intimate might be going on between the two.

Suzanne had extremely peculiar ideas about what kind of music the St. Louis audience would accept. It was not unusual for her to program "two-fers" by Michelle Shocked or "The Swinging Steaks" in morning drive. In the meantime, Ken and Suzanne were out with the record company weasels three or four nights a week. And as they were being wined and dined, they were also agreeing to deals that had the station playing music by completely unknown artists. They even stuck a ridiculous promotion on the air, in which some "lucky listener" would win a live concert by Sonia Dada in their living room. The station received three entries. Most of us were of the opinion Ken had given Suzanne the station to play with; unfortunately, that meant they were both playing around with our careers.

We all did the best with what we had to work with. It wasn't much. Even so, our morning show registered a healthy increase in the ratings. We considered it a miracle, since about the only place the station could be heard was in cars.

In January of the following year, Steve & D.C. were rehired by the new owners of the station they'd been fired from. Strangely, the local press really backed off from the intense vilification it had subjected the duo to resulting from the highly publicized racial slur the previous spring. Now it was being characterized as a "mistake" or "error in judgment" when, in fact, there had been a dozen or more episodes the press had failed to pick up on. I knew the two were back, because their first day on the air, they persuaded about a dozen of their die-hards to call in on cell phones while they circled our building, beeping horns and generally acting obnoxious.

"Why target J.C.?" you might ask.

Good question.

As far as anyone's been able to surmise, the pair was convinced the only way they would be able to assume the top position in morning radio was to somehow get rid of me. The two's direct assault on my image with their dirty tricks and stunts had begun as far back as 1992. They made crank calls at all hours of the day and night, even during the months when Laura was pregnant with our first child. Over and over again I'd answer the phone. Over and over again the caller would listen without saying a word. However, I could usually hear the faint sound of Steve & D.C. talking in the background followed by the electronic "burst," which only a radio station telephone "interface" system produces at the beginning and the end of a call. I knew it was Steve & D.C.

I never thought I was dealing with an intelligent pair here. But one morning after I'd received about a dozen calls spread over a twelve-hour period, I drove to their station and met with their general manager. I told him I wanted the harassment to stop. All *that* confrontation did was to make the two angrier.

My daughter, Addison Clark Corcoran, arrived on May 3, 1993. Within days of her birth, Steve & D.C. began making Addison the butt end of dozens of creepy jokes. Upon seeing her photo in the paper, D.C. referred to her on the air as a "mongoloid baby." My wife and I had just been blessed with a beautiful, healthy baby, yet we were receiving letters and cards expressing sympathy over the birth of our "handicapped" child. When I began hearing the name "Addison Clark" used repeatedly on their show, I realized they had re-named their intern with my daughter's name.

Coming after me was one thing, but coming after my baby daughter was another. Friends and family began asking me, "What kind of business are you *in*?"

The Steve & D.C. racial slur had taken place during my stint at KMOX, which proved simply too attractive of a scenario for the local press not to interview me about. Each time I said what I believed: The two disc jockeys had blown the bottom out of the genre of unrestrained, unpredictable FM morning radio.

The press had fallen in love with the term "shock jock." As miserably pathetic as it may seem, I think they liked it because it rhymed. Now anyone on the air who was doing more than just time-and-temperature was tagged with the moniker. But reporters who used "shock jock" or "shock radio" in their stories about me were quickly corrected. I had interviewed "celebrities" like Tom Eagleton, Leslie Stahl, Art Buchwald, Ted Koppel, Dana Carvey, Mel Gibson, Steven Spielberg, Bob Greene, Dr. Benjamin Spock, John Goodman, and Steve Allen. I had done live broadcasts from Moscow, London, Washington and New York. I had confronted issues like music censorship, suicide and the Gulf War. I had been part of a team that had raised money for a dozen local charities. Nobody in my own industry would ever have dared to characterize what I did as "shock radio." I insisted we had raised the standard on FM morning radio. Steve & D.C. had now sent it crashing to the ground.

Radio consultants relish the thought of having clients whom the audience believes will say "anything." But here's a little secret: We announcers want the audience to **believe** we'll say "anything." It's just an illusion; we don't really say "anything."

But here were two guys who, apparently, would.

And so, when Steve & D.C. returned to the air, I became the primary focus of daily, and in some cases, hourly attacks. They spoke of places they said they saw me where I'd never set foot. They spoke of behavior they'd witnessed that never occurred. And still, ninety-nine percent of the time I ignored their outrageous behavior.

Most of what the pair would perpetrate against me were stupid, kindergarten-level antics. A cash prize was awarded to the winner of a contest who could write a song portraying me in the most negative manner. One morning, a box of doughnuts was delivered to us at the station. A few minutes later a call came into the Steve & D.C. show; the caller claimed to have dropped the doughnuts off to us but not before rubbing them on his ... yes, you **may** think the worst. A thousand dollars was offered to anyone who could produce a tape of me being a jerk to them. Essentially, their station was offering money to its listeners to stalk me.

Finally, an incident occurred that I could no longer remain silent about. It involved their show and the death of a friend.

We'll never know if KSDK chief meteorologist, Bob Richards, was guilty of harassing a woman with whom he'd allegedly had an affair.

But as soon as the rumors first surfaced, Steve & D.C. seized the opportunity. Though the two would later indicate the woman in question contacted them, allegations emerged that the station's producer tracked the woman down and offered to give the woman the chance to tell her side of the story on the air. When the woman's account of his alleged infidelity literally exploded in the local media, Bob tried to dismiss her story as the ranting of a crackpot viewer. Days later, Steve & D.C. allowed the woman to air answering machine messages she claimed Bob had left her. Now, all of St. Louis was hearing another side of the extraordinarily popular weatherman, family man, telethon co-host, husband and father.

The phone in my office at home rang at about 3 a.m. It was Matuschka. Authorities had not officially confirmed the victim's identification and no specific details had been released to the press, but everyone on the scene knew it was Bob's plane that had taken off from Spirit of St. Louis airport earlier that evening. The plane had risen steeply, nose-dived, then crashed into the ground in a fiery explosion.

All the local television and radio stations had waited for the official word from police and the coroner before reporting that the crash involved Bob, so when we took to the airwaves three hours later, I had the unenviable task of informing our city that it had lost a friend. Trish Brown, our meteorologist and one of Bob's direct competitors on television, fought back tears as her voice broke.

On the air, I did not even try to hide my rage. Stunts are stunts. Fun is fun. Publicity is publicity. I didn't want to trivialize Bob's life by reducing our discussion to a form of grandstanding, but now a man was dead. "Is this really what we're here for every day?" I wondered.

A number of our callers indicated they felt Bob had gotten what he had deserved. "Interesting logic," I concurred. "Now an appropriate punishment for alleged infidelity is death. I guess half of our professional athletes, business leaders and politicians ought to be executed."

However, my outspoken anger and hostility over this senseless tragedy merely served to escalate Steve & D.C.'s vindictive behavior toward me.

Representatives from St. Louis' Cerebral Palsy Foundation came to us with an idea called "Brats on the Lot," which would feature a special, live broadcast on the lot and lawn in front of the Regal Riverfront Hotel downtown prior to a Cardinal game. During the event, we'd encourage listeners to buy a bratwurst and drink, with all proceeds going to the foundation. We went on the air that Friday evening at five, complete with a set of wireless microphones, which allowed us to roam several hundred feet from the central broadcast area.

I was across the street in front of the stadium garage east when it happened. In the middle of a live conversation with a group of lot attendants, a man jumped out of the crowd and collided with me on my blind side. Then he fell to the ground, appearing to go into convulsions. Completely startled, I backed away, signaled the station to return to music, and hurried back across the street and away from this "psycho." I was talking about it with other station employees when one of our account executives ran up to me yelling, "It was D.C.!"

Though I was convinced she was mistaken, I looked across the street and saw the man who had jumped me standing next to D.C., both laughing in an exaggerated fashion. When he saw he had my attention, D.C. pulled out a cell phone and demonstratively dialed a three-digit number, presumably 911. Moments later, the area was overrun with police and squad cars with flashing lights. D.C., the man who had jumped me and friends of the two, swarmed around the officers, one of whom just happened to be our producer and co-host, Karen Kelly's, husband, of the St. Louis Police Department.

Over the course of the next few minutes, I overheard several officers saying they were about to take me to jail. Finally, after close to forty-five minutes of discussion, argument, accusation and counter-accusation, the guy who jumped me and I were arrested and charged with peace disturbance. Sunday morning's *Post-Dispatch* carried a page-two story describing the altercation, along with a notation that I had been unreachable for comment. For any of the million-plus readers of the Sunday paper, it appeared as though J.C. Corcoran had instigated a street brawl.

The story did, however, identify Tim Melton as the man who had jumped me. When I began checking around to see if anyone could provide me with information as to just who this guy was, it quickly became clear: Tim Melton was the intern who was using my daughter's name, Addison Clark, on the air. And the dirt got even better. Lia Nower, a longtime personal friend of Steve Shannon and D.C. Chymes, had written the story in the *Post-Dispatch*.

The next morning, Steve & D.C. spent most of their show recounting the incident. As one would expect, in their version I was accused of "attacking" their intern, whom they said was too weak from the experience to come to work or to the phone. They claimed that I struck Melton, "knocked him to the pavement and repeatedly kicked him in the ribs causing injuries that required five hours of hospital attention."

Given the escalating level of their provocation, I wondered what might come next. Would they pay a woman to come to my hotel room on a road trip in the middle of the night and scream "rape?"

Later that week I held a news conference to announce my $2.5 million lawsuit against Tim Melton, D.C. Chymes and Zimmer Broadcasting, parent company of their radio station.

The *Riverfront Times* printed an expansive story about the case, complete with Melton and Chymes' absurd accusations. *RFT* columnist Richard Byrne sarcastically offered his services as a "lack of character witness" on my behalf, and insisted the whole thing was a publicity stunt on my part because, quoting Chymes, "his ratings are low."

(Unbelievably, in a subsequent *RFT* column, Byrne took a swipe at my daughter **by name**. As reprehensible as I found this, when I visited the paper's office the following week, hoping a man-to-man discussion might stop Byrne's propensity to add fuel to a bonfire, Byrne refused to come to the lobby. The next day, Mary Ellen Owens, who co-hosted The Point's morning show across the hall from our station and who knew Richard, told me he said he believed I'd come to his office to "beat me up." In my mail slot I found a nasty fax from Byrne expressing his outrage.)

Personally, these events were taking a terrible toll. And professionally, things weren't going much better.

River City Broadcasting, through a bizarre change-of-ownership shift in the television market, was about to become an ABC TV affiliate and, thus, required massive changes in their physical plant at Tucker and Cole. Because the station would now have to assemble an entire news department, the entire floor below us would be destroyed and converted into a newsroom and studio. For the next six months, we did our morning radio show with the sounds of drills and jackhammers in the background. The project was delayed for weeks when asbestos was discovered in the walls, forcing the company to hire men in helmeted "moon suits" to "safely" remove it. We knew it was being "safely" removed because we could watch them **through the holes in the floor of our studio**!

It became abundantly clear River City's radio properties were now being seen as little more than a promotional "tool" for the new television operation. We knew they'd planned to run tons of free commercials for the Channel 30 news on both the "River" and the "Point," and that the radio budgets would be slashed. I also knew that since Mike Bush worked at KSDK, and Trish and I worked at KMOV, it wouldn't be long until this arrangement would become an "issue." Channel 30 would want to promote their own news personalities, not those of their competitors.

We'd also had to make a change in the show's co-hosting duties from Matuschka to Channel 30's quick-witted, entertainment guy, Tom Brown. He and I had occasionally run into each other covering entertainment stories for our respective television stations, and he had just begun to take some of the movie studio junkets in L.A. and New York that I'd had to pass on due to my new, family considerations. I was beginning to cut back on the number of out-of-town, weekend trips, so I helped Tom out by introducing him to all my Hollywood contacts and field reps, believing he could begin going on the trips and interviewing all the movie stars I no longer could.

The station brought in its fourth program director. Soon after, the third general manager in less than two years was brought in; a woman who had earned a reputation for being tough, often unnecessarily so, in her previous job at KMJM (Majic 108). And with all of it came a change in the radio station's format and name. In the fall of 1994, "The Fox" became "The River," and converted from rock to something called Adult Album Alternative, characterized by lots of music written by seriously pissed-off women.

And there was an equally bizarre development involving Channel Four. Remember the story about the woman back in 1987 who canceled all of the Schnucks advertising upon hearing KSD had hired me? Well, one day she was paraded into the KMOV newsroom and introduced as the station's new marketing director. One of her first acts was to pull meteorologist Trish Brown off our show, and put her onto one of our competitors.

I was getting the idea this woman didn't like me.

But I was also beginning to believe my new boss, Linda O'Connor, did. In fact, after a few months of "observing" me, Linda took me to lunch at the St. Louis Club to inform me she was planning a massive advertising campaign to change my image. "You're not the pariah people think you are, J.C.," she said. "Nobody's done anything to offset all the awful publicity you've been beaten up by for years."

With only a few months left on my contract, this was exactly the kind of support I wanted to hear. Even with the station's failure to make good on the original promise to move the broadcast tower so that our signal was competitive, we were doing very good work and our show was the only thing producing any ratings success on the entire station. Now I felt as though I was about to cash in on a little of that success.

But a few days later, Linda dropped the bomb that, in exchange for the marketing push I'd be getting, she expected me to accept a salary freeze. I rejected her proposal, and Linda barely spoke to me again. Instead, she began "wallpapering" us (an industry term used when a boss issues memos for every imaginable infraction, presumably, to try to build a file against an employee). I recall one memo ordering us to refrain from using the phrase, "big ass." (The term was currently in vogue, thanks to David Letterman's ala "Big Ass Ham.") But my protests no longer mattered; I was persona non grata with my new boss. When Linda started in on Karen, things really began to get ugly.

Karen and I had no choice but to abandon one of the best ideas we ever had, The Breakfast Club "Cabinet." With the incredibly diverse cross-section of listeners we had, we thought having one "expert" in every imaginable field would serve both comedic and practical purposes. We intended to give each individual selected an intentionally bureaucratic-sounding title. For example, a local lawyer became "Attorney General." A local mathematics teacher was given the title "Secretary of Slide Rules." One openly gay listener was dubbed "Administrator of Alternative Lifestyles." We had already staged an impressive "swearing-in" ceremony at the St. Louis Science Center, but with no budget and no support from the station, this outstanding idea never realized its potential.

It was about this time that I began experiencing serious back trouble again. I went in for a second surgery in March of 1995, but not before having a long series of discussions with Tom Brown about the possibility of leaving St. Louis as a team. We'd really begun to gel and, at the urging of some close friends in the business, I hired an agent out of Chicago for the express purpose of getting me back to my hometown.

Karen and I had been broadcasting from Chicago the previous fall when the NFL owners meetings were being held and St. Louis' fate as an expansion franchise city was being determined. Chicago suddenly looked great to me again, and its disappointing radio stations seemed to offer a lot of potential. With things looking so bad in St. Louis, the Windy City looked like a place where Tom and I could clean up. Though she was to represent us as a "team," it was I who paid all $2,500 of Lisa Miller's upfront fee for her to represent Tom and me.

It wasn't until a few weeks later that I learned my reward for *that* generous gesture was for Tom to return to The River's management and rat on me. He told them I was looking to leave, and he'd be more than willing to take over the morning show at the station for a handsome raise when I did. Karen and I had to look at Tom every day for three months, knowing full well that he had sold us out. Finally, in the spring of 1995, the "River" pulled the plug on me with two months remaining on my contract. Tom got the show. Karen and Mike Bush departed shortly after. It would be more than another full year before the station's broadcast tower was moved. General Manager Linda O'Connor was replaced about two years later.

About the only positive thing to come out of the experience at the "Fox" and the "River" was our meeting up with air personality Vic Porcelli. Our changeovers at ten every morning became somewhat legendary, and spawned a feature that we still do today called "The List," an assemblage of weird non sequiturs uttered on the show each day.

In February 1993, nearly three years after Y98's Karen Carroll had filed her slander suit against us, St. Louis Circuit Court Judge Robert H. Dierker Jr. dismissed the case. In doing so, the judge made reference to our on-air comments about Carroll as "little more than puerile name-calling" and, he continued, "stated simply, it is modern broadcast journalism at its best."

But with all that had transpired, I arrived at the conclusion that my time in St. Louis was over.

Postscript: *My daughter, Addison Clark Corcoran, admittedly has an unusual name. As a kid I'd been close to my grandfather whose middle name was "Clark," and I'd always thought that would make a good name for either a girl or a boy. We'd also been toying with "Allison" and "Madison," when I suggested combining the two into Addison, remembering I'd liked it as Bruce Willis' character's last name on "Moonlighting." But now we were looking at the names "Addison"* and "Clark," which is the precise street location of Wrigley Field in Chicago where I'd spent some of the happiest, most memorable days of my life, and a place I consider to be the most beautiful on earth.

"Never throw anything out."
–Talk Show Host Johnny Carson

Chapter 25

It was the spring of 1995. Laura was pregnant and I was out of work.

I spent most of that summer traveling around the country on a series of job interviews my new agent had set up. I quickly caught on to the fact that the whole thing was a wild goose chase. Jobs didn't even *exist* at the majority of stations I was being sent to. And, most important, I now wanted a job in Chicago. Finally, *"Partridge Family"* star-turned-felon-turned-talk-show host, Danny Bonaduce, was preparing to launch a syndicated television show, and we learned his slot would be opening up on WLUP (The Loop) in Chicago where I'd worked in the late seventies. All my interviews went well and it appeared I had the best shot at the job. Then, Bonaduce surprised everyone by announcing he'd continue on the radio show in addition to performing his new gig on television.

I was losing faith in my agent, Lisa, and I turned back to Jeff Gershman. According to the terms of the contract with Lisa, Jeff still had jurisdiction over my affairs in St. Louis. Predictably, Jeff went straight to those whom I would have considered the least receptive. After several meetings with KSHE produced very little, Jeff contacted Karen Carroll, who was overseeing KSD-AM, KSD-FM and Y98. After several weeks of discussion, Carroll revealed she'd been toying with the idea of moving Frank O. Pinion to KSD-AM and returning me to the KSD-FM morning show. She had just brought in a new program director, Steve Brill, whose name I immediately recognized. Brill had interviewed for the job when I was at KSD a few years earlier, but had been quickly dismissed upon indicating the first thing he'd do upon being granted the position would be to "put the clamp on J.C. Corcoran."

But our meetings went very well despite what I found to be an amazing coincidence. You'll recall the fierce rivalry and intense dislike (make that "hatred") which existed between my high school, St. Laurence, and Brother Rice. And you'll recall my initial reticence about going to work for KSHE's Rick Balis, a Brother Rice alum. Now, unbelievably, Steve Brill also identified himself as a product of Brother Rice High School. A thought flashed across my brain: These Brother Rice guys are coming back to haunt me.

Eventually the color came back into my face and, on the last Wednesday of November of 1995, Alan Box, president of EZ Communications, flew to St. Louis for the contract signing of J.C. Corcoran at KSD and the renewing of the contract of Guy Phillips at Y98. That same morning my wife went into labor.

The signing was set for three o'clock at the KSD/Y98 building on the far, west end of downtown. Since Laura's contractions were still pretty far apart, she suggested I sign the contract and return home so that we could go together to the hospital. I reminded her that I'd have my cell phone with me at all times.

Things got started late and took much longer than I'd anticipated. I still hadn't heard anything from Laura, so around four o'clock, I took my cell phone out of my pocket to give her a call. But as I went to dial the number, I noticed the "no signal" indicator was lit. What I didn't know, having never been in the building before, was that it was constructed of steel and concrete, and thus, impenetrable. I rushed outside and frantically placed a call to Laura, who said the contractions were coming faster; she was loading the car as we spoke. I hauled ass down Highway 40, exited at McKnight and skidded into our driveway eleven minutes later. We arrived at the hospital just after 4:30 p.m. Whitney Elisabeth Corcoran was born less than two hours later.

The following morning I made a brief appearance on Guy Phillips' morning show to make the official announcement of my return to KSD. The next day, December 2, 1995, "J.C. and The Breakfast Club" with Karen Kelly, KSDK's Mike Bush, KMOV's Jamie Allman, Lance Hildebrand with traffic and Eric Mink on television debuted on 93.7 KSD.

Three days later, KSHE General Manager John Beck announced the signing of the "Bob and Tom" syndicated morning show.

"Hollywood is like high school with money."
—Actor Martin Mull

Chapter 26

By this time, my skills as a morning host and my knowledge of the entertainment industry had begun to dovetail. Certainly, when it comes to traditional or hard news, I can't even carry Charles Jaco's microphone case. And though he's not really considered "local," the guy who personifies broadcasting perfection to me (as well as a million others) is, without question, Bob Costas.

But, when it comes to the kind of avant-garde interviews that require a certain level of entertainment within them, I now felt that I could go stride for stride with anybody in town. (Of course, if you do anything long enough you stand to get pretty good at it. In my case, I had been fascinated with the art of the interview since the age of six, when I began pestering Chicago television and radio personalities to see how they did it.)

I've witnessed a lot of things backstage at various shows and concerts, in locker rooms, and on television and movie sets. My father was a fan of a 1960s documentary in which comic Shelly Berman (who used to close his show with a somewhat poignant routine portraying one side of a telephone conversation) had his act interrupted when a phone located just offstage began ringing. The program showed Berman going into a rage over the incident, none of which was within earshot of the audience he'd just performed for. It was an early heads-up as to the difference between what a person is onstage and what a person is offstage; clearly an intriguing theme, and one which I would later see repeated a hundred times in my career.

Backstage at a "Kiss" concert in 1977, I watched as the individual members of the band, each a mile high in enormous platform shoes, had Polaroids taken of topless women dangling from their ... well, I think you get the idea. I walked with Rodney Dangerfield as the comedian, dressed only in socks, shoes and a robe, nervously paced, periodically peeking through the curtain in an attempt to determine the demographic make-up of the crowd. Peter Frampton must not have been expecting us in his dressing room since he was wearing only scivvies, which displayed a gruesome-looking, thirty-inch scar that traversed his torso, the result of a near-fatal car accident he'd been involved in years ago. I assisted Nicole Kidman in removing a piece of blueberry muffin from between her teeth moments into a television interview we did together. I watched the difference in Sam Kinison's personality from the first time he played St. Louis to the time he came in a year later complaining that "the eleventh commandment is 'Thou Shalt Not Be Hipper Than Lorne' (Michaels)." I walked into a dead-silent dressing room of "Heart" at a time when rumors of widespread personality conflicts swirled around the band, and Nancy Wilson confided that her little dog she traveled with was "the only thing keeping me sane." And I stood, dumbfounded, as an emotionally-incapacitated Brian Wilson ingested more drugs than I'd ever seen in my life while two prostitutes, one black and one white, draped themselves over him minutes before he was to take the stage.

Whenever possible, I asked celebrities to pose for a photo with me, though things are usually quite rushed at that point. Oftentimes, the next reporter is being ushered in, tapes are being exchanged, lights and cameras are being adjusted, and a scene resembling switching classes in high school takes place.

Following a late-eighties interview with Morgan Fairchild at the Chase Park Plaza, I handed my camera to a production assistant and quickly hopped up out of my chair to pose with the blonde beauty. But as I went to put my arm around her, I found her tiny waist and torso to be half the girth I was expecting. This miscalculation resulted in me accidentally putting my arm **all** the way around her; my right hand landed squarely on her right breast (which, by the way, was au natural). After an embarrassing moment or two during which we both sort of let out an awkward giggle, we attempted the pose again ... which produced the identical result!

One interview I never got to do was with country music's Eddie Rabbitt. He'd obviously read one of the negative pieces in the national trade papers about the FCC fine I'd incurred after the Jessica Hahn, *Playboy* incident in the late eighties and felt compelled to write me a hate letter—on official, gold-embossed, Eddie Rabbitt stationery. He died a few years ago, without giving me the chance to thank him.

"Television is a vast wasteland."
—Former FCC Chairman Newton Minnow

Chapter 27

Though radio has always been my first love, I got an indescribable kick when working on television. In many ways, television "legitimized" me in the eyes of the media. There has been a vast difference, however, between my first few years on the tube and my last.

When I was added to the KSDK newsroom staff in 1985, working in television provided an incredible rush. The station was making a fortune, a fact reflected in the amount of money it spent. If you could justify it, Channel Five wrote the check. I was able to go almost everywhere and do almost everything I pitched. That meant everything from live shots along the red carpet at the Grammys in L.A., to covering the bar-hopping scene on St. Patrick's Day. And just being around pros like Dick Ford, Deanne Lane, Bob Richards and Mike Bush allowed me to learn from the best.

Budget cuts were being announced with alarming regularity by the time I exited the station in the fall of 1991. If it hadn't been for the talented, friendly people in the newsroom, going to KMOV would have been a real come-down for me. The place looked like it hadn't been painted since the Eisenhower administration, the equipment was in a state of decay, and there was no source of natural light in the entire place. But I concluded the more spartan-like environment might make me a better writer.

Ah, the art of writing.

Virtually every major player in the day of television's infancy came from the newspaper industry and, thus, writing was paramount. My mentor at KSDK, Ava Ehrlich, recognized my writing ability early on and made me work on it that much harder. But as the years passed the emphasis on good writing diminished, and video replaced the written word. "Television without pictures is radio," they cried. In my last few years in a television newsroom, I can remember painfully few instances in which a discussion about content wasn't obliterated by a more "urgent" discussion about style. Although some reporters were excited about their story, the majority of them were often more interested in showing off their stand-up (the portion of a taped story during which the reporter delivers a short adjoiner on-camera).

Consulting firms began swooping down on the hundreds of television stations across the country to work their "magic," which often consisted of changes to the news set, adjusting the lighting, or positioning the anchors closer to one another. At KSDK, the wooden tabletop at the anchor's desk was "fixed" by replacing it with glass.

But what about the *news?*

Watch your favorite ten o'clock news program tonight. Add up the commercials, teasers, promos, chatter during the toss from news to weather and news to sports, lotto numbers, kickers and other filler and you'll find less than a third of the show is comprised of "news." And during rating sweeps, the banter is much worse. There's always at least one station in each market that's adopted the cynical policy, "If it bleeds, it leads."

Television news has become all about style. It's entertainment. Or, in the words of singer Don Henley, "When it's said and done they haven't told you a thing." And if the product itself has been cheapened, then the manner in which the product is delivered has been completely devalued. Here's a news promo I heard a few days ago: "Significant changes in our temperatures. We'll tell you whether that means up or down tonight at ten."

Can't you just tell me it's going to get hotter or colder **now**?

Over an animation of a plethora of enormous asteroids on a collision course with earth and the news' theme song, one station, as it headed into a commercial break, actually said, "And, are asteroids about to hit the earth? We'll have that story coming up."

Of course, if the destruction of civilization were imminent, the story would *naturally* come about eight minutes into the newscast, right? It reminded me of the famous, 1967 George Carlin routine:

Bulletin! Bulletin! Bulletin!
Bulletin! Bulletin! Bulletin!
Bulletin! Bulletin! Bulletin!

Here is a bulletin, bulletin, bulletin. The sun did
not come up this morning. Huge cracks have appeared
in the earth's surface and big rocks are falling out of
the sky. Details in twenty-five minutes on Action
Central NEWS!

The television industry likes to blame its sneaky promotional tac-
tics on the increased availability and use of the remote control. And
while that excuse has some merit and the remote has been a factor in
the adjustments stations have had to make to remain competitive,
most of the new breed of television news producers likes the faster,
slicker, flashier news style. And they're good at it, too. Regardless that
most of it is journalistically bankrupt, of course.

Fewer and fewer television newsrooms believe legitimate entertainment coverage is worth the money anymore. But there was once
a time when they did.

I began taking part in movie studio press junkets in 1985. When I
started, the process was clean, efficient and beneficial to both the
studios and the local television stations. Although, from the description I'm about to give, it may not sound like it was.

Twenty or thirty weekends a year I'd board a plane for L.A. or
New York after the radio show on Friday morning. I'd then grab a
cab to a four-star hotel, where I'd pick up my press kit at the hospi-
tality suite for that night's screening. The suite, incidentally, always
featured a massive spread of deluxe meats, vegetables, breads, fruits,
pastries, desserts and beverages. Around six I'd board a bus, along
with reporters from dozens of other cities who were there for the
same reason. We'd arrive at a specially reserved theater or screening
room where we'd view the film (but not before being handed a cer-
tificate good for free popcorn and soda). After the movie, we'd be
shuttled to a club or restaurant for a private dinner party and entertainment and, later, back to the hotel. The following morning, after a
top-notch, room service breakfast, round robin television interviews
would begin. The stars of the film would each be set up in a fully-
decorated and professionally-lighted suite, complete with two cameras, one trained on the star and the other on the reporter, and a full

crew of technicians to manage the operation. Two videotapes were inserted into the decks, a director counted you down and, for the next six to eight minutes, you were one on one with a real live Hollywood star. At the end of the interview the director handed you your tapes, and it was off to the next suite. Two or three hours later, a studio representative would come along with your amenities: a handsome duffel bag emblazoned with the title and logo of the film stuffed with T-shirts, caps, key chains, stuffed animals, drinking glasses, boxer shorts, mugs ... well, you get the idea. I even got a pewter beaver once.

Did I mention all this was free?

Of course, the obvious question becomes, did any of this unsolicited "generosity" raise ethical issues for a reporter? The answer is both yes and no.

When a movie studio releases a new film, a negative review from a local critic is the least of its worries; its biggest concern is a lack of awareness by the potential audience. So although I'm sure the studios *preferred* receiving favorable publicity, what they really wanted was for the reviews—good or bad—to get on the air. Eventually, however, the studios got greedy.

During the thirteen years I participated in junkets, this issue of studio control over its film reviews and celebrity interviews became more pronounced. When I first started traveling for the movie studios in 1985, most of the reporters invited were just that: reporters. As time went on, however, these experienced, formally trained journalists and individuals were replaced by "junketoids," who held the deliberately ambiguous title of "talent." Now it was the twenty-two-year-old producer of "Bill and Bob's Wacky Movie Show" showing up for the weekend junket. Half the new people arriving on the scene looked as though they'd been hatched in a Petri dish in a secret laboratory at MTV. More and more, the studios were figuring out that they could have greater control over what was being said about their movies by inviting television "personalities" instead of reporters to promote their movies. (I'd like to describe these "personalities" as having compromised their integrity, but most had none to begin with.)

In 1990, while I was still with Channel Five, I had to begin fighting with the studios about Channel Four, which had just hired an entertainment reporter named Dawn Meadows. Dawn was a sweet girl who had just returned to St. Louis after working in television out of town for several years, and was now attempting to horn in on my territory. One afternoon I was monitoring Channel Four's 5 p.m. news when I saw a promo for an upcoming interview I didn't know Dawn had done. As I watched the piece, I saw what looked like a male hand flash into the frame from the interviewer's chair. When I rolled the tape back and hit the freeze frame, sure enough, it was clearly the hand of a man.

After doing some digging, I discovered that Dawn had not even been on this particular junket, and had evidently asked another reporter for a "dub" of his tape (who was apparently unaware that his hand had flashed on-camera for an instant). This, of course, was all well and good except for the fact Dawn was passing off this interview on Channel Four as one she'd done herself. The deception was soon exposed in the *Post-Dispatch*.

By the mid-1990s, the studios were beginning to lean away from preserving the already-fragile boundaries ensuring journalistic ethics and heading toward infecting the entire process with promotional and marketing overkill. It was a climate that eventually spawned the "quote whores"; a label given to the numerous "junketoids" who were now saturating the movie industry's promotional market. Often from smaller markets or less important shows, the "quote whores" would gladly trade saccharine, upbeat quotes the studios could use to promote their movies in exchange for the studio's guarantee they'd be given access, sometimes special access, to the stars. Regardless of whether the movie was good or bad, even a bad movie could be made to look attractive when one of the multitude of "quote whores" raved, "Funniest comedy of the decade!" or "I laughed, I cried, I ruined my seat."

The greediness continued. Now, instead of one or two sets of movies and interviews a weekend, as many as four or five sets were being crammed into a two-day period. It was not uncommon for me to conduct twenty or more interviews on a single trip to L.A. And in order to make it all fit, many of the interviews were being cut to as short as four minutes.

As the system became infected with the new breed of junketoid, the professional interviewers were now viewed as nuisances, and their numbers in the system dwindled. The combination of now having a beautiful family and the increasing unpleasantness of the junket system, greatly eased my decision to cut my involvement by more than half.

But it's not as though I didn't have some remarkable memories.

"I get nostalgic for the time in my life before I was an empire."

—Madonna

Chapter 28

I'd clearly reached a point where fewer and fewer celebrity interview opportunities were producing the kind of thrill I used to get. Politicians, particularly incumbents or those on the campaign trail, proved to be the worst guests. Professional athletes tended to be smug. The majority of rock stars and musicians turned out to be so disappointing that I found myself thinking I was more interesting than half the celebrities I was interviewing. (The director of *Two Days in the Valley* apparently found me so entertaining during our interview that he asked for my card and whether I was interested in doing any acting!)

The Hollywood studios are notorious for baiting reporters with the promise of interview opportunities with huge, mega-stars, only to have those stars pull out of their commitments once the press arrives.

With the much-anticipated release of the film *Evita* came word that Madonna would, in fact, participate in the junket. I thought that because it was Madonna, and since she had just given birth to her first child a few weeks ago, she might cancel her junket before I arrived in L.A. In spite of my misgivings, I did my research anyway and arrived in L.A. on a Friday afternoon in December 1996. Arriving at the Ritz-Carlton in Marina del Ray, I found myself being escorted into a large room in the hotel basement. In the adjoining suite, the pop-music queen had been answering questions from members of the press since early that morning.

The atmosphere was completely different from any interview situation I'd ever experienced before. (With the possible exception of

Paul McCartney in Las Vegas in 1993. His security was overtly on display, and a grimace of concern was etched on anyone involved in the staging of the event.) I was briefly "interrogated" by a member of Madonna's imposingly large security staff. When he seemed satisfied that I harbored no hostility or malevolence toward his client, I was ushered to yet another room even farther into the hotel's bowels, where I would be placed on-deck. Finally, it was my turn.

She sat in the sort of ornate, oversized chair I'd only seen in fancy hotel lobbies. A state of bedlam existed just outside her door, but this new mother sat serenely; almost suspiciously calm amidst the jungle of wires, cables, lighting umbrellas, cameras, tape decks, audio equipment, technicians and studio personnel. A single, thin wire led up from the floor, around her thigh, behind her back, under her arm and onto a lapel on her dress where it attached to a tiny, hidden microphone. It looked as though it might take an hour to re-set everything to its proper place had she stood up.

Madonna was dressed in an incredible skin-tight, gold gown with red highlights, cut low to highlight the performer's world-famous bosom. Her hair and make-up were perfect. I recall thinking how much more beautiful she looked than I was expecting. I scribbled the word "radiant" on my notepad.

After exchanging brief pleasantries, the production assistant interjected with the usual set of questions pertaining to my choices of camera shots, which was quickly followed by a countdown and cue to begin the interview. I was to have six minutes with Madonna.

It's usually hard enough to determine what areas you can afford to cover with a celebrity, particularly a notable celebrity, in so little time. But this was Madonna! Where could I *begin*? How, in six minutes, could I possibly cover the career of the most-controversial, pop-music icon in history? Here sat a woman who had nearly monopolized the entertainment industry for a decade. She had won a role that had been coveted and vied for by over half the major actresses in Hollywood and, in the process of making the film, had subjected herself to intense public scrutiny and an incredible amount of pressure.

As I began to form the words of my first question, we plunged into total darkness.

For the next few moments there was absolute chaos.

Numerous security people swarmed into the room. Some were armed with flashlights, nervously fanning the lights in a swirling disco pattern. A few of the guards even eyed me, as if to suggest this might be more than just a typical, garden-variety power-outage and that I might have had something to do with the outage. It wasn't until I counted at least a half-dozen, extremely large men in dark suits talking into their sleeves, that I realized just how many undercover personnel were actually involved in the security effort to protect this woman. (Keep in mind that each of those six guys was talking to someone else!)

In the following five minutes while the scramble to restore power ensued, Madonna was offered every beverage, amenity and accommodation the hotel and movie studio could conceive of. She politely declined their efforts and, since she was nearing the end of her daylong interview schedule, she remained seated, assuming, like everyone else, that the lights would be back on any second. When they still didn't come on, two flashlights were placed on the floor nearby. Eventually the room emptied out and, for the next twenty minutes, there I sat, in the dark, face to face with a woman who was, arguably, one of the most-famous people on the planet, without so much as a single recording device in operation. Now, instead of a formal interview, Madonna and I found ourselves killing time by chit-chatting.

She told me she had never been to St. Louis. In attempting to characterize our town as conservative, I remembered what had happened after Madonna had released her infamous sex book. KEZK, in one of the true grandstanding moves of our collective lifetimes, ran newspaper ads touting the fact that none of her records would be played on their "family-oriented" station. (They had gotten gobs of publicity a year earlier when they pulled the same stunt following the Michael Jackson scandal.) Her eyes widened as I proceeded to give her the details.

Having lived in her home state of Michigan in the seventies and, having vacationed in the fashionable Harbor Springs area in the extreme northern tip of the state for a few years, the topic turned to a rumor that had been making the rounds. I had heard that she was building a house not far from the area where Laura, the kids and I had stayed for several summers, which also sported the vacation homes of Michigan natives Bob Seger, Tim Allen, and others. She told me she'd heard that rumor, too, but it wasn't true; she did, however, occasionally visit her father in the Traverse City area.

Not surprisingly, her face lit up when we spoke of her new baby, Lourdes, who was only a few months old. She seemed more than willing to discuss the fact the baby was still breastfeeding, though I got the distinct idea that might have been coming to an end soon. With the holidays only a few, short weeks away, I told her how mushy I'd gotten around the time of my daughter's first Christmas, and asked if she thought she'd do the same. She said she was looking forward to the time when Lourdes could actually open up a gift. "Right now I can't stop shopping for her," she said. "For now, though, I buy a present, I wrap it, I unwrap it, and then she grows out of it in three weeks!"

We covered every imaginable subject in that twenty-minute period before the lights came back on. Then, following a crush of activity from the make-up, hair, lighting and video brigade, the interview we had tried to record earlier was finally underway. I thought I detected a hint of a silly grin on Madonna's face as I asked my first question; a tacit acknowledgment that we'd already done our best work together. Still, she spoke of the five-page letter she'd written to director Alan Parker practically begging him for the role, and how she identified with Eva Peron, a woman who, on the outside, seemed to gush self-confidence, but who actually was consumed, at times, with self-doubt.

Because Madonna has participated in hundreds and hundreds of interviews since she burst onto the music scene in 1983, she may not even recall the events of December 13, 1996. But it's one of my favorite stories.

She's also someone whose dilemma I can identify with. In the mid-eighties, Madonna re-created the famous production number from the Marilyn Monroe film, *Gentlemen Prefer Blondes*, for her video of the song, "Material Girl." Over the years, I've seen dozens of negative stories about her, clearly written by producers with *Hard Copy*-like, hostile bent, beginning with some variation of the dismissive lead, "Well, the 'material girl' is at it again..."

But the whole *point* of that video was to illustrate that confusing the person and the performer is usually a mistake, and that show business is all about illusion. Nobody seems to remember that after Madonna grabs all the diamonds and manipulates her way through the legion of adoring men, the "Material Girl" video ends with that same girl, out of costume, leaving the soundstage and going home with the guy in the old, beat-up, pick-up truck.

In that regard, I can certainly identify with Madonna.

Because once they lay a label on you, good luck trying to get rid of it.

"The best kind of person to interview is someone who has an axe to grind."

—Talk Show Host Larry King

Chapter 29

The first, real celebrity I ever interviewed live, on the air, was actor Chuck Norris. In 1978, he came through Fort Wayne, Indiana, on a promotional tour for his film, *Good Guys Wear Black*. And for the next twenty-plus years since that day, I've done hundreds of television and radio interviews with celebrities.

Certain images stand out. So here, in no particular order of importance, are some of the impressions I've culled from sitting across from the "not-always-so-rich-but-at-least-fifteen-minutes'-worth-of-famous" people. Each of the star's names is followed by the number of times I can recall having interviewed them, along with some of their projects that brought us together.

Kevin Costner, *Waterworld, Revenge, The Postman;* (3)

Although friendly and genuinely interested in giving a good interview, each of the three times we've spoken I've noticed a level of intensity which he, himself, seems uncomfortable with.

Julia Roberts, *Something to Talk About;* (1)

Pretty, smart. Looks exactly the same in person as onscreen. Very guarded.

Tom Hanks, *Punchline, Joe vs. The Volcano, Saving Private Ryan;* (3)

Smart, funny, insightful. Terrific command of the language. Everything you hear about him is right. He's too good to be true.

Dustin Hoffman, *Wag the Dog, Outbreak, Ishtar;* (3)

Surprisingly playful. The last three interviews we did bordered on silly, though he firmly believed *Wag the Dog* was serious, Oscar material.

Adam Sandler, *The Waterboy*; (2)

Extremely unassuming and polite. Once he gets rolling, he appears to be similar to the spaz he portrays in his films which, by the way, he cares about very much.

Eric Clapton, *Hail! Hail! Rock & Roll: A Tribute to Chuck Berry*; (2)

Given his close calls with death and the fact many of his contemporaries are no longer around, he seems glad just to be alive at this point.

Richard Gere, *Primal Fear*; (1)

About what you'd expect. Handsome, well dressed, smart. Sort of "out there." **Very** Hollywood.

Bill Murray, *Scrooged, Quick Change*; (4)

Rarely in what many would call a good mood. Razor-sharp wit, but acts like he's doing you a favor by displaying it.

Jerry Seinfeld, Fox Theatre, Westport Playhouse, 1990 Grammys, KSHE In-Studio, (5)

Became increasingly arrogant as his star rose. One of the most unfunny people you'd ever want to be around. Turns it on for the camera. Turns it off the rest of the time.

Harrison Ford, *The Fugitive, Presumed Innocent*; (2)

Extremely guarded, but capable of displaying a near silly side. Dead-serious about his craft and his privacy.

Helen Hunt, *Twister*; (1)

The diametric opposite of the roles she tends to play. A very tough edge. Looks like she could beat the crap out of you. Didn't seem very happy the day we spoke. I got the distinct impression there might be a lot of those days.

Mike Myers, *Wayne's World, Austin Powers, SNL* cast party; (3)

Boundlessly polite. One track of his mind always on work and sort of jumpy about it. Haunted by rumors he's difficult to work with. Constantly referred to his wife, Robin. Really wants his movies to be creatively funny and respected.

Michelle Pfeiffer, *Dangerous Minds*; (2)

Much more waif-ish than I expected; not the drop-dead gorgeous beauty I expected, either. Very smart. Barely changed facial expressions the entire ten minutes during each of our two interviews.

Bill Pullman, *While You Were Sleeping, The Zero Effect*; (2)

One of the most charming leading men I've ever met. Very nice, down-to-earth guy who really likes to laugh. One of my favorites.

Spike Lee, *Do the Right Thing, Jungle Fever, Mo' Better Blues*; (4)

What you see is what you get. Smart, opinionated, fairly good-sized chip on his shoulder. Dead serious when he told me he doesn't believe the AIDS epidemic's disproportionate attack on people of color is a coincidence, and that the government might have something to do with it.

Jamie Lee Curtis, *Halloween H2o, Tell Me Again About the Day I was Born*; (2)

A real pistol. Smart, funny, pretty, fashionable, professional, lots of personality. Adores being a mom and a wife equally. Loves cutting-up during interviews.

John Goodman, *Punchline, King Ralph, Fallen, The Big Lebowski*; (10)

Unquestionably one of the nicest people I've ever met in or out of show business. This man will never forget who he is or where he came from.

Drew Barrymore, *Everyone Says I Love You, The Wedding Singer*; (2)

Like a modern-day hippie or love child. Very smart, literate and well versed. Kissed my hand at the end of our first interview. Friendly as the day is long.

Dolly Parton, *Steel Magnolias*; (1)

One of the most beautiful women I've ever met. Her skin was indescribable.

Henry Winkler, *Memories of Me, The Waterboy*; (2)

One of the nicest, gentlest men I've ever met. Even when I ran into him in the hotel hours after our interview he remembered my name and asked if I thought he had done a good job. Truly ironic that he's nothing like the character that made him famous.

Melanie Griffith, *Pacific Heights*; (1)

Dumb and obnoxious. Tried to tell me what questions I could and couldn't ask her.

Billy Crystal, *When Harry Met Sally, Father's Day, Throw Mama From the Train*; (4)

Funny, genuine and warm—as long as he's in a good mood. During his stand-up comedy days, he was known for calling comedians he believed were stealing his jokes.

Pamela Anderson, *Barb Wire*; (1)

Knock-down, drag-out beautiful at the seven-month mark of her pregnancy. Knows what she thinks about things and expresses herself well. Traces of a childlike quality.

Gene Siskel, "Siskel & Ebert at The Movies"; (10)

I can't begin to describe how much I learned from Gene. Probably because of the power he commanded, many in the industry didn't like him and he'd frequently appear grouchy. For some reason, though, he took a liking to me and always gave me a sensational interview. Hardly a week goes by that I don't think of him.

Sandra Bullock, *While You Were Sleeping, A Time to Kill, Practical Magic*; (3)

What you see is what you get. One of the few stars who is as sweet in person as she appears on-screen. Honest to a fault, beautiful, funny. The best.

Woody Allen, *Everyone Says I Love You*; (1)

So frail looking it looked like a strong wind could sweep him away. Intimidatingly intelligent. Appeared oblivious to the fact that many of his movies had a profound effect on people.

Jodie Foster, *Nell*; (1)

Much, much tinier than appears on screen. Beautiful! So smart you could practically hear the hum of microprocessors coming from her temples. Could have talked to her all day. Incredibly appealing.

Leslie Nielsen, *Naked Gun*; (3)

Full of the devil. A very, very sweet man.

Cameron Diaz, *Kingpin*; (1)

A scrawny, barely attractive ditz.

Danny DeVito, *Throw Mama From the Train, Get Shorty*; (2)

A charming man whose passion for his work and enthusiasm for life in general is completely contagious. You can see a very shrewd mind at work if you ask the right question.

Michael Douglas, *Fatal Attraction, The Game, Falling Down, Indecent Proposal*; (4)

A bit on the slick side, but likeable and funny. Likes to fool around in interviews. Really knows what it means to give a good interview and how that skill helps the projects he's involved in.

Robert Downey Jr., *Soapdish*; (1)

We spoke at a time we now know was very difficult for him; regardless, he seemed like a very strange, low-life kind of guy. Told me he considers acting a male occupation.

Albert Brooks, *Defending Your Life*; (1)

Having been a huge fan for so many years, I was worried he

might not live up to my expectations. He did. Almost exactly what I'd hoped he'd be. Very funny, especially in that sort of neurotic way. Thoughtful and intelligent. One of my real heroes.

Super Dave Osborne, *Super Dave*, Grammys; (3)

Such a funny, likeable man. Picked me up and took me to breakfast one morning in L.A., and showed me Aaron Spelling's mansion, which was under construction, on the way back to the hotel. Like his brother, Albert Brooks, Osborne is one of my real heroes who has shown wonderful friendship and support over the years. I can't believe I'm in the position to be able to just pick up the phone and talk to this guy after having idolized him for so many years, particularly during his days with "The Smothers Brothers" television show.

Richard Dreyfuss, *Always*, JCCA Book Fair; (2)

Absolutely electric. Though our interview went extremely well, I got the idea he only needed about three percent of his brain to answer my questions. A brilliant talent and an exciting person to listen to.

Oprah, *Beloved*; (1)

Very driven and confident. Thinks she's a little funnier than she really is. Much nicer and more personable than the posse of women who surround her.

Cameron Crowe, *Singles*; (1)

As the inspiration for *Fast Times at Ridgemont High*, the director of *Jerry Maguire*, and now *Almost Famous*, I was delighted to find him such a down-to-earth, affable guy. Extremely thoughtful, intelligent and observant. Absolutely loves his work. A real sort of "seventies" dude.

Dennis Miller, *The Rants*, Westport Playhouse; (8)

Best writing on television. But like opening a box of Crackerjack–you never know what you're going to get. Occasionally personable, funny, doing his best to give you a good interview. More often he's cranky, unnecessarily combative, and a pain whose butt you have to kiss to get anything decent. I have no clue what triggers his mood swings.

Don Henley, Musician; (2)

Guarded, but after he sizes you up and decides you're OK, utterly fascinating to talk to. Smart guy with opinions about everything from politics to farming.

Whitney Houston, *The Preacher's Wife*; (1)

Six months pregnant at the time of our interview, she was radiant and demure, elegant and classy. Moments after the camera was off I heard her yapping like a Ricki Lake audience member.

Bruce Willis, *Die Hard*; (3)

Does not suffer fools. Not particularly fond of the press and will, on occasion, attempt to intimidate. Sizes you up quickly and communicates with you using that grading system. Can be very funny on occasion.

Demi Moore, *Striptease, Indecent Proposal, The Scarlet Letter*; (3)

Beautiful, fit, smart. Acted as if she might want to show her humorous side but uncomfortable about doing so. Seemed like she was carrying the weight of the world on her shoulders.

Sylvester Stallone, *The Specialist*; (1)

Friendly, funny; smarter and more insightful than he gets credit for. Seemed distracted, like he had a lot on his mind. Shorter than you'd think.

Dana Carvey, *Saturday Night Live*; (4)

One of the most talented performers I've ever met. Loves performing but could easily do without the business part of it. A genuinely nice guy.

Michael J. Fox, *For Love or Money, Doc Hollywood*; (2)

Complex. Funny, smart and constantly looking for ways to entertain himself.

Arnold Schwarzenegger, *Junior*; (2)

Friendly in a businesslike way. Funny. Works the hype on what he's promoting at the expense of showing his human side. Shorter than you'd think.

Cindy Crawford, *Fair Game*; (1)

Pretty, intelligent, friendly, down-to-earth and genuine. A lot more going on in there than you'd think. Very cognizant that she's from DeKalb, Illinois.

Steve Martin, *My Blue Heaven, L.A. Story*; (5)

Polite, extremely intelligent but occasionally distant. Makes almost no attempt at being funny offstage. Many interviewers and fans come away crushed after meeting him.

Dan Rather, CBS News; (1)

The diametric opposite of what I was expecting. Gushingly accommodating, friendly, genuine and warm. We spoke on the set of the CBS *Evening News* ninety minutes before air in the midst of absolute chaos, yet he made me feel as though we were the only two people in the room.

Meg Ryan, *When Harry Met Sally, Courage Under Fire*; (2)

Sweet and pretty, friendly and warm ... and yet, hounded by stories that there are two Meg Ryans.

Robin Williams, *Cadillac Man, Father's Day, What Dreams May Come, The Birdcage*; (4)

If you start an interview in serious tone, Robin will give a serious, intelligent interview, displaying staggering depth as a person and a performer. If you start the interview upbeat, Robin becomes a wild animal, peppering his responses with incredibly filthy, exhaustingly funny routines, voices, impressions. Unique. Brilliant.

Salma Hayek, *From Dusk til Dawn, 54*; (2)

One of the most naturally beautiful women I've ever met. Not a rocket scientist but not claiming to be one, either. Funny.

Bill Cosby, Fair St. Louis; (1)

Quite a bit darker personality than his onstage persona but a charming man.

Andy Rooney, *60 Minutes*; (1)

Much friendlier, funnier and more personable than I had heard. Longs for the good old days.

Denzel Washington, *Courage Under Fire, The Preacher's Wife, Fallen*; (3)

One of my favorites. Absolutely full of the devil. Personable, intelligent and thoughtful. Loves to laugh hard. The best. I will see anything he's in.

Melissa Etheridge, In-Studio; (1)

A favorite. Overall presence makes her one of the most appealing women I've ever met. Very funny and smart. Completely dedicated artist. The best.

Eric Stoltz, *Memphis Belle, Two Days in the Valley*; (2)

An extremely gifted actor who, I believe, will accomplish something great some day. Also a combative individual who practically picked a fight with me during an interview. A real head case.

George Clooney, *Batman, The Peacemaker*; (3)

As appealing as you'd imagine. A real movie star. One of the most naturally funny actors I've ever met. Understands giving good interviews is part of the job. The kind of guy every man would like to have as his best buddy. In a position where he could be a total jerk but isn't.

Jackson Browne, The Fox Theatre; (2)

A real jerk. What a disappointment.

Roseanne, Westport Playhouse; (2)

Someone who's been allowed to act so bizarre for so long that she doesn't even recognize how weird she is. Directed her displeasure at me for ten minutes when the airline lost her luggage. But John Goodman told me he's never seen anyone fix a script more efficiently.

Mel Gibson, *Lethal Weapon 2, Air America*; (2)

Much funnier than people know. Tends to shut down if not proud of the movie he's in. Really does love *The Three Stooges*. Not tall.

Charlize Theron, *Two Days in the Valley*; (1)

Seemed as though she had a lot on her mind. Looking perfect at all times a very low priority, a quality that made her that much more appealing. Looks to have everything to be a huge star.

John Travolta, *Get Shorty*; (2)

A real movie star. I practically detected an aura around him. Incredibly magnetic personality. Fastens his eyes directly on yours for the duration of the interview. The real thing.

Kim Basinger, *My Stepmother is an Alien, Batman*; (2)

Incredibly attractive and appealing and, paradoxically, almost tomboy-like. Radiant. Funny. Embarrasses easily. Somewhat jumpy. I think most men would sell their mother in exchange for a weekend with her.

Kevin Spacey, *GlenGarry Glen Ross*; (1)

An actor's actor. A very dry sense of humor bubbling just beneath the somewhat serious surface. Sharp as a tack.

Annie Lennox, Musician; (1)

Called me a nasty name after I asked why she seemed to enjoy being portrayed in a negative light. Takes herself entirely too seriously.

Yasmine Bleeth, Actress; (1)

Breathtakingly attractive. Playful and funny. Soooooo cute!

Edward Norton, *Everyone Says I Love You, Rounders*; (1)

Intense. Very intense. Incredible talent.

Nicole Kidman, *Batman, Portrait of a Lady*; (2)

Possibly the most beautifully-statuesque actress I've ever met. This woman was just stunning! Extremely playful.

Leonardo DiCaprio, *The Basketball Diaries*; (1)

Seemed like sort of a punk. Pretty busy trying to look cool. Another surprisingly non-descript talent.

Robert Redford, *Quiz Show*, filming of *The Natural*; (1)

Thin and fit and with extremely "weathered" skin. Surprisingly approachable and down-to-earth. Strong command of the film-making process and extremely sure of himself without acting arrogant. Really wants the projects he's involved in to count for something.

Gwyneth Paltrow, *Valmont, Shakespeare in Love*; (2)

Very sweet and polite. Much more down-to-earth than you'd expect. Very thin and surprisingly plain. Sensational actress.

Marilu Henner, Actress and Author; (2)

Bubbly, vivacious and effervescent in public. Arrogant, noisy and bitchy offstage. A real pain.

Sela Ward, *54*; (1)

One of the most attractive, fortysomething women I've ever met. Sweet and playfully funny. What a babe!

Bill Maher, *Politically Incorrect*, Westport Playhouse; (2)

I never miss his show, but this guy is one of the most arrogant jerks in the business, and I can remember him being that way as far back as the mid-eighties when I emceed a comedy bill he was on. Just impossible, even when you're kissing his ass.

Phil Collins, "Genesis," *Buster*, The Arena; (4)

On those rare occasions when he wasn't having marital problems, he was friendly and almost a silly kind of funny. Brilliant artist. Very introspective at times.

David Letterman, *The Late Show with David Letterman*; (7)

The first time I interviewed him via phone in 1985, David insisted we talk for a half-hour before I rolled the tape; an unprecedented request for me. Seemed genuinely interested in me, my show and the goings-on in St. Louis. He enjoyed our last face-to-face interview in New York so much that we ran fifteen minutes over. Frightfully thin. Very much wants to do a good job. He speaks fondly of his days in local television and, privately, will acknowledge he could easily still be in that position himself. Dave's my hero.

Jay Leno, *The Tonight Show, The Fox Theatre, Westport Playhouse*; (10)

Though he's been extremely gracious with his time over the years, Jay's act has begun to grate on me. His monologues used to consist of brilliant writing, subtle nuances and common experiences. Now they're just loud. Regardless, I owe him a debt of gratitude for how much he contributed to the show, often coming into the studio on Saturdays, to be on the air with me. Gets little credit for having an incredible mind. This is a bright guy.

Natalie Portman, *Everyone Says I Love You, Beautiful Girls*; (2)

Made me wish I were eighteen again. One of the most-talented, young actresses I've ever encountered. Like Reese Witherspoon, shows maturity well beyond her years. We might be looking at the next Meryl Streep here.

And special recognition goes to...

D.L. Hughley, "The Hughleys"; (0)

In this ABC situation comedy, a young, black family moves into an upscale neighborhood, only to find their ever-present fear of racism is unwarranted. We liked the premise so much, we signed up for a ten-minute satellite interview "window." Minutes before it was our turn, a producer called to say Mr. Hughley had decided to speak only to the black radio stations.

Michael Moore, *Roger and Me, Pets or Meat, The Awful Truth*; (0)

Michael has scheduled a combined total of six radio and/or television interviews with me over the course of the past decade and has failed to show for any.

"Pretty soon, everything will be one thing."
—Reporter Jamie Allman

Chapter 30

I f my career in St. Louis up to December of 1995 could have been described as "unusual," then it was about to drift into the surreal.

The fallout from the FCC's 1992 ruling allowing multiple-station ownership was just beginning to rear its ugly head. All across the country, companies were buying one another up at a pace to beat the band.

Karen Carroll, the woman who had sued me a few short years earlier, was now my boss. My program director, Steve Brill, was yet another alum of my high school's arch-rival. And I was saying the name "KSD" again.

This time, though, the station's slogan was "Killer Classics and Today's Best Rock." So now along with "Freebird," "Layla" and "Satisfaction," we played new songs from Alannis Morrisette, Collective Soul and Melissa Etheridge. The new format was viewed as a chancy approach at best by the company. And when the ratings didn't show an immediate increase, station management pummeled Brill into altering the musical presentation; a process we would see repeated with frightening regularity over the next two years. In all, no less than six "re-positions" of the musical format were forced upon us. KSD's audience couldn't tell from one month to the next what the station was supposed to be. What made the situation all the more maddening was the fact that these forced changes were being handed down by the very people who had screwed the station up in the first place, and who had proven themselves to be the least qualified to be playing around with it now. On more than one occasion our operations manager, who oversaw KEZK, Y98 and KSD-FM, even suggested that a conversion to a "smooth jazz" format might be more beneficial to the company.

Though the station struggled overall, the morning show posted regular gains in our target demographic of 25 -to 54-year-old males. As part of a conscious effort on my part to confound our competitors—nearly all of whom were predicting a Hiroshima-like, cataclysmic explosion within hours of my new relationship with Carroll—I kept my dealings with her "light, bright and tight" at all times.

Seven months into what was proving to be my second, successful stint at KSD, I took my family on vacation to Michigan. On our second day there, I received word that our three-station group had been sold to a company based in Boston. The Chief Operating Officer of American Radio Systems was John Gehron, the same man who had attempted to lure me to WLS in Chicago ten years ago. ARS prided itself on being a "blue jeans and leather jacket," employee-friendly company. Not long after the sale, a plaque bearing the company's mission statement was hung in our hallway. Point number one: "Grow people faster than assets."

Most of us believed our sale to ARS would prove beneficial to KSD. Y98 was the adored pet project and first love of Karen Carroll, and always got the best of everything. KEZK, meanwhile, had been a cash cow for years. Both stations programmed female-based, soft pop music and had relatively low overhead. Their respective staff looked well scrubbed and conservative.

But since its collapse following my departure in 1991 and subsequent abandoning by Gannett less than two years later, KSD had fallen out of the top ten and was considered the poor, problem, bastard stepchild. And we were a *rock* station! We weren't like the other boys and girls. We dressed weird and some of us had funny hair.

"*Eeeeeeeeeiiiiiiuuuuuuuuuuuuu!*"

This was also my first encounter with Karen Carroll's unique managerial style. Instead of the standard-issue Grateful Dead or Rolling Stones' posters that adorned the walls of every radio station I'd ever worked at, Carroll's policy of "approved artwork" meant only a few, framed, nondescript etchings were allowed. We might as well have all been working at an insurance company. Her policy even limited the number of family photographs we were allowed to display in our cubicles. And, given the fact that this was a radio station, the edict that no radios were to be allowed on any employee's desk seemed odd, to say the least. To say there existed a wide distance between management and staff at the Market Street location of KEZK, Y98 and KSD AM and FM might best be illustrated by Carroll's propensity to refer to her employees as, "the help."

This was also my first experience with one of the most backward philosophies I'd ever come upon. The concept of attempting to make money via the operation of a radio station wouldn't seem to be a complicated one. Just find a "hole" in the market, program music to fill that hole, hire some prominent on-air talent to execute the format and entertain the audience that gravitates to it, plan some catchy promotions, promote the hell out of the place and run a couple television commercials once in a while. Raise the advertising rates each time the station's ratings increase, and your sales staff shouldn't have much trouble generating revenue. It's not brain surgery.

But under the Karen Carroll system, the entire dynamic centered on the sales department. In fact, what came out of your speakers at home or in your car was viewed as incidental. I'd like to explain this philosophy in more detail, but I didn't understand it then, and the logic of it has failed to develop over time.

In fact, I've often spoken of the fatal flaw that exists within the world of professional broadcasting. It's inconceivable that a coach or manager of a professional sports team, for example, could possibly ascend to such a position without ever having played the game. But the sad truth is that the overwhelming percentage of radio station general managers, the people who are charged with the responsibility of determining what you get to listen to each day, somehow arrive there with little or no broadcasting experience. In truth, they get there by being successful sales people. Consider, if you will, a shoe salesman at your neighborhood mall. One day a buddy tells him of an opening in the sales department of a suburban newspaper. From a position selling ad space, he moves on to a larger newspaper. After maxing out at that job a year or two later, another pal might convince him that, if he can sell ad space in a paper, he'd be much happier making more money selling airtime in radio. After a few years, he's promoted to local sales manager at the station. Then he's promoted to national sales manager. Finally he gets to run the station. Part of his duties include making decisions; such as whether your former favorite station continues to play Eric Clapton-type music, or is now going to convert to elevator music. He also gets to decide whether J.C. Corcoran will continue to work at the station, or whether he can find a cheaper, more innocuous host to take J.C.'s place.

The most dangerous part about the system is that these managers usually think they know something about broadcasting simply because they have the job. For these people I offer my "brick-laying" analogy.

If you asked most people whether or not they could build a brick wall, I'm fairly sure the majority would answer "yes." They might do a good job for a while, and they might even look pretty good doing it. But when it came to doing the corners, the window openings, doorways and leveling, they might have to admit the procedure is far more complicated than it had first seemed. The same analogy could be applied to morning radio. Truthfully, it isn't that hard. But this doesn't mean it's easy, either. If it were, there would be a lot more people who sounded good doing it.

But as long as we're being truthful, I don't believe the job of radio sales is always easy, either. That's probably one of the reasons why I've gotten stuck wasting so much of my time over the years sidestepping salespeople armed with cheesy, dopey and, in many cases, just plain stupid ideas for commercial endorsements. In fact, one KSD sales woman I worked with holds the record for the most idiotic schemes in a three-week period. It all started with her pitch to me on a proposal she'd put together for her new client, a hair replacement company. I politely explained that I had no interest in having someone drill holes in my head and stuff them with hair. (Can you imagine the reaction I would have received if I had walked up to her with the idea to pitch breast implants?) A few days later, she approached me with a plan for me to go bungee jumping on the air. Again, I calmly asked if she recalled seeing me around the station in that giant, plastic neck brace following the spinal fusion operation I'd recently undergone. Bad move on my part. The following week she walked in looking for my OK on a deal to broadcast from an MRI machine, blissfully unaware of the fact that I had needed a whopping fifteen milligrams of valium to offset the claustrophobic horror of being confined to its coffin-like environment prior to my surgery. Finally, she came up with the perfect pitch: the Dent Wizard.

I'd accidentally backed into my garage door earlier that year and dented my car. So when she suggested a segment featuring the Dent Wizard removing the dent from my car during a live broadcast from the station's parking lot, I was glad to say "yes." But the day before this was to happen, the account executive in question showed up in the doorway to my office with a concerned look on her face. "The Dent Wizard looked at your car in the parking lot yesterday, and the dent is in a place where they can't get at it," she reported. When I broke the news to her that there was no point in continuing with the plan for the scheduled segment, she frantically requested I give her some time to "work on it." She returned a few hours later with her solution. "The Dent Wizard has offered to put a dent in your car door and then take it out," she offered with a thoroughly unconvincing Kathie Lee Gifford-like bounce in her voice.

Though it wasn't widely reported, I chopped that saleswoman into small pieces and buried her remains in a field behind the station.

Indeed, the only thing worse than bad sales people are bad sales people who know they have the station management's blessing to roll right over you. Thus was the case at Karen Carroll's Market Street location of KSD. After several sales managers quickly came and went, a red-faced, four-hundred pound fellow I'd known briefly from my first stint at KSD was put in charge of the station's sales effort. The last words he and I had exchanged concerned his travel agency's treatment of several contest winners from our show. Assured that they would be placed in a "Hollywood" hotel as part of their grand prize package, the winners used the word "horrifying" to describe their hotel's conditions. Not long after this fiasco, I was held up at the airport when it turned out his agency had stapled my boarding passes to the wrong tickets on a flight to Chicago.

I was not thrilled to see him again.

For two years, almost hourly fights erupted over our out-of-control sales department's usurping the station's programming effort. Big screen televisions "delivered just in time for the Super Bowl" were arriving in contest-winners' homes months late. KSD on-air personalities regularly had to go to hell and back to get paid for weekend appearances at car dealerships, shoe stores and the like. Stupid commercials and promos were turning up on the air without anyone's approval.

As usual, problems were worse for me since I'd had a long-standing policy against involvement with dubious clients like casinos, fireworks stands and, especially, the diet industry. In fact, during the late eighties and early nineties, I was the only major on-air talent in St. Louis not doing live endorsements for an imperious, overly-aggressive diet company that would eventually be cracked by the federal government for shady business practices. Many just took the money and ran. Ethics often has a way of disappearing quickly under a green-and-white carpet.

Again, to be fair, our account executives were under tremendous pressure to recoup the annual $3 million price tag on the St. Louis Rams' broadcasts. It would have been difficult enough even before the team's habit of winning a game only in the months when a solar eclipse was predicted. But what was going on at KSD between sales, programming and management was something entirely different. If I hadn't known better I would have sworn they were trying to make us fail.

Little did I know.

Of course, every time sales failed to make budget, news of another cutback came shortly thereafter. Everyone was asked to double-up on ion duties. This, of course, was going on while Y98 and KEZK led the good life. As if to rub our noses in it, through the glass of the conference room we could see their weekly staff meetings were being catered. We got vending machines.

Still, we had our moments. In the fall of 1996 KSD engineered a deal to give away a new $180,000 house in southwest St. Louis County. At the culmination of the three-month-long contest, six finalists gathered at the Trans World Dome for the chance to claim the grand prize. During the halftime of a Rams' football game, the mini-home was wheeled out to the fifty-yard line and the finalists were brought onto the field to see which of the keys they held would fit the front door.

I grabbed the microphone to begin the festivities.

"Hello, everybody! I'm J.C. Corcoran from The Breakfast Club on 93.7, KSD!"

"Booooooooooooooooooooooooooooo!!!!!"

Hmmm. Sixty-six thousand people who had been drinking since eight o'clock that morning and they **still** knew who I was. Was I big in this town or what?

And there was "St. Louis Night" at the *Late Show with David Letterman*. Three, full planeloads of fans of the show, many of them who had won tickets on our show, were going to fill the Ed Sullivan Theater in New York for an extravagant Friday night taping designed to super-serve the St. Louis market. I helped whip up the nearly five hundred-audience members into a frenzy by documenting their three-block walk from the hotel with my television camera crew. Then, once inside, I kept the excitement level high with a series of audience participation games, all of which was recorded and sent back to St. Louis via satellite for KMOV's ten o'clock news. Dave was clearly amazed by the thunderous, elongated response when he walked on stage that night. So much so, that comedian Eddie Brill (who performs the audience "warm-up" each night prior to the taping) recently told me that Letterman's staff still refers to that night as having set the standard by which all subsequent audiences have been judged.

The rush we all got from those events subsided quickly upon our learning that yet another sale of our group of stations was imminent. This time we would not fare as well. CBS/Infinity, the company that owned KMOX, announced its plan to purchase American Radio Systems, the company that had just purchased us. Rod Zimmerman, the manager who had pulled the plug on me at KMOX, would be my boss again. Zimmerman couldn't have been in a very good mood following the recent mega-defection of Bill Wilkerson, Wendy Wiese, Kevin Horrigan, Jim Holder and others to KTRS. (He'd even recently whacked the blind guy with Tourette's syndrome.)

The stress level in our building was off the scale. I recalled a psychology course I'd taken in college in which two rats were placed in a cage together. The rats seemed to get along and appreciate each other's company. But when two more rats were added to the cage, all four rats began to fight. And when the temperature was raised and food and water withheld the fighting became even more vicious and, occasionally, even the rats ganged up on one another.

As the KSD contingent got pushed further and further to the periphery of the Market Street location, many of us began to feel like the caged rats. I also discovered a perverse appreciation for an animated feature developed by *Beavis & Butthead* creator Mike Judge for *Saturday Night Live* called, "Milton." Milton was a low-level clerk confined to a cubicle somewhere in a nondescript office building who is browbeaten into submission by his passive/aggressive boss who wants to store huge boxes in his tiny work area. (The animated short would later be made into one of the greatest movies of all-time, *Office Space*.)

As if we needed more problems, nagging scheduling issues with KMOV forced us to part company with co-host Jamie Allman, and although the affable veteran Mark Klose stepped in nicely, Jamie's quirky presence was missed, and his departure sent a ripple of instability through the show.

While all this was going on, there was trouble brewing at home. Laura and I had decided to move from our home in Ladue to a more family-friendly environment in Brentwood. We also decided to move into a house that we needed to almost completely rehab. Now, instead of arriving at "home-sweet-home" each afternoon, I walked into a dusty, noisy construction site with no kitchen, running water in only two rooms and electricity in less than a quarter of the house. Laura and the girls were staying with friends so, each night after saying "goodnight" to my family, I was in the unenviable position of sleeping by myself in what looked like a gutted abode in Beirut.

A nagging throat condition, which was causing me to lose my voice on a regular basis, was eventually diagnosed as a throat nodule, most likely stress-induced. I began attending massage and voice therapy sessions three times a week in an attempt to avoid surgery and relieve the problem. I was also advised to go "cold turkey" on caffeine; I had been drinking as many as ten cokes a day.

In the meantime, Karen Kelly had been involved in a series of discussions with management about getting more airtime and more money, but the talks had produced extremely mixed results. The station was willing to expand her role, contingent upon her performing two newscasts in the five o'clock hour each morning. This stipulation required her to get up even earlier for work, and gobbled up the time normally spent on last-minute preparations for each day's show

Karen was miserable. I was miserable. The situation was miserable.

One morning Karen and I had an ugly fight. Things were never the same. Karen left the station a few months later. Now I was out one producer, one co-host ... and one best friend.

A few weeks later I was driving to work on highway 40 in the middle of a blinding rainstorm when I began to hydroplane. At a speed of about sixty miles per hour, my car spun completely around twice and angled toward the shoulder. It was only by the grace of God that I wasn't killed.

I did a lot of soul-searching those next few weeks.

Before the big sale of KSD and the other two stations in our group ever transpired, the new owners called us into a meeting to reveal an even more diabolical development. While they looked forward to reeling in Y98 and KEZK, they noted the acquisition of KSD would put them over the government's ownership limit.

Bill Murray's motivational speech from *Stripes* began echoing in my head.

"*We are the wretched refuse. We're mutts.*"

"*So, then who's going to own us?*" I asked.

"*Well. Nobody.*"

"If you come at me with a fist, I'll come at you with a brick."

—*Spin* author Michael Sitrick

Chapter 31

I t had been an exhausting six months.

Almost three years after the highly-publicized altercation that led to my lawsuit against Steve & D.C., the case finally came to trial. On a cold, rainy Monday morning in a musty court building at Market and Tucker, a jury was picked and we began making our case. Two brilliant attorneys, Steve Ryals and Gary Snodgrass, represented me. Tom Caradonna, the lawyer who defended "Guns N' Roses" lead singer, Axl Rose, in his infamous Riverport Amphitheater "stage-diving" assault case, represented Steve & D.C.

We had rejected their out-of-court settlement offer when they wouldn't guarantee that my daughter's name, Addison, be permanently removed from their show. (Truthfully, this was all I really wanted at this point.)

A jury of twelve men and women listened for six days as both sides hurled accusations back and forth. But damning evidence began to mount against Steve & D.C. It was revealed that as many as ten people from their station's staff took part in planning the assault, that one of their station vehicles was involved, and that there were gaping holes in their version of what had really happened. On day three, Tim Melton, the intern who had used my daughter's name on the air (in addition to jumping me, faking a serious injury and then, with Chymes, filing a false police report) was reduced to tears as attorneys Ryals and Snodgrass brutalized him on the witness stand.

Closing arguments were given on the sixth day of the trial, A little over an hour later, a unanimous jury awarded me a combined total of

$370,000 in actual and punitive damages.

To this day, the *Riverfront Times* has yet to acknowledge this verdict.

Postscript: *A few months later, a young black woman approached me on a MetroLink platform and asked if I was J.C. Corcoran. It was Nicole Hammonds, the object of Steve & D.C.'s infamous, racial diatribe. We shared a long hug.*

"It's not paranoia if they're really after you!"
—Director Woody Allen

In learning KSD would not be included in the sale to CBS, we were also informed we would have to leave the building. KFNS, the AM all-sports station, announced it was vacating its facility across from Union Station and arrangements were made for us to move in. A bizarre plan was struck for CBS (the company *not* buying us) to continue loosely overseeing our operation until a new owner could be found. Our paychecks, we were told, would be mailed to us from a law firm in Boston. On our first day in the new building, our entire air staff ceremoniously pummeled and destroyed the plaque the American Radio Systems had hung in our hallway when they purchased us, which read: "Grow People Faster than Assets."

Although the new building was very nice, the equipment was a joke. Someone identified the main control board in our studio as the one KEZK had tossed out more than ten years ago. CD players didn't fire. Microphones didn't work. Tape decks were out of alignment. The tape cartridge machines should have been tossed on the scrap heap ages ago. Listeners were subjected to regular bouts of "dead air." All the engineers and technicians were still at the Market Street facility, and there was little interest on their part in helping us fix the growing list of malfunctioning equipment. After weeks of literally pounding on a module that was shorting out in the control board, the module finally burst into pieces one morning during our show. I later learned the control board we were using had been rejected by the "Broadcast Center" several years prior as part of a donation effort.

We also lost ace traffic reporter, Lance Hildebrand, in the process.

His departure meant our show had experienced more than a fifty-percent overhaul. Karen, Jamie and now Lance were replaced by young John-John Canavera in the producer role, with Mark Klose co-hosting and reading news and an amusing young guy named John Brown in the traffic chair. We tried our best but, given the circumstances, it wasn't enough. Program Director Steve Brill (who had lost both his mother and father unexpectedly within the previous one-year period) fought each day for the survival and dignity of his troops. But it couldn't have been clearer—KSD had been left for dead. We had no budget, staff, promotions, decent equipment, stationery or business cards, and found no pleasure in what we were doing.

The ratings began to fall. Steve Brill announced he was getting a divorce.

A few months later, rumors began to circulate that one of the largest, most-aggressive companies in broadcasting, Jacor Communications, had its eye on KSD. A charge of adrenaline bolted through the station. A new general manager arrived one day with promises of big things to come. We rallied around him.

Three months later he was gone.

I was in California on the *Saving Private Ryan* studio junket when I received a call from my father: Mom had had a mild heart attack. She was being airlifted to a larger and more sophisticated hospital than the tiny facility near the rural Wisconsin home they had retired to a few years before. I flew back to St. Louis on the red-eye, but as I was hurriedly tossing a change of clothes from one travel bag to another, Dad called to say Mom had passed away.

While I was in Wisconsin at Mom's funeral, the managers at the Market Street location instructed their engineers to raid my office. They removed a CD-making machine, along with a few other pieces of equipment they claimed were theirs.

Things were moving fast. Within days of my return from the funeral, the formal announcement was made that Jacor was, indeed, purchasing KSD. We figured our long nightmare was about to end. Another new general manager was introduced to the staff. Again we heard of big things to come. But at a staff meeting one day, I got the distinct impression that something ominous was about to happen. My lucrative contract was due to expire at the end of the year, and even though our morning show remained the strongest entity the station had, I still felt "vulnerable."

I decided I was going to make it impossible for the new company to look past us. I would again have to prove myself. I signed on for every movie junket, every interview opportunity, every personal appearance and every chance to shine. The combination of Mark, John, Schlanger, Eric, John-John and I was starting to sound very good on the air. I sensed we had turned a corner, despite the state of total decay the rest of the station was going through.

St. Louis' star-studded, "Planet Hollywood" grand opening was a project I'd been working on for over a year, and my efforts ensured that KSD practically owned the event. We were able to give away dozens of special VIP passes on the air. I also co-hosted the pre-show in front of forty thousand viewers with St. Louis native Todd Newton of the "E!" entertainment network, and reported live on Channel Four's ten o'clock news with interview segments featuring celebrities like John Goodman and Bruce Willis.

Over the course of the next few weeks, I presented one-on-one interviews with Tom Hanks, Steven Spielberg, Oprah, Jamie Lee Curtis, Chris Rock, Rene Russo, Robin Williams, Yogi Berra, Sandra Bullock, Roseanne, Adam Sandler, Don Rickles, Richard Simmons, Yasmine Bleeth, Richard Dreyfuss, Norm MacDonald and Billy Bob Thornton. And I did the show from the Blockbuster Video blimp several hundred feet above downtown St. Louis.

While all this was happening, a guy by the name of McGwire was making history down at the ballpark. Partly out of love of the game and partly because KSD's previous budget cuts meant the absence of a sports reporter to gather locker-room sound bites, I did that job, too. On Labor Day, KSD had lucked into having the entire "Big Mac Land" section in Busch Stadium's left-field terrace for listeners and staff. Almost before we had gotten settled in our seats, Mark McGwire tied Roger Maris' regular season home run record with a shot off the Stadium Club glass less than twenty feet below us. We could all be seen, openmouthed, on the front page of *USA Today*'s sports section the next morning.

The following night my friend, former Cardinal pitcher Greg Mathews, invited me to dinner at the Stadium Club with him and a few of his pals. Those pals turned out to be a group of a dozen or so guys like Chris Pronger, Geoff Courtnall and Kelly Chase of the St. Louis Blues. We all watched and cheered as homer number 62 disappeared directly under us. In the pressroom after the game, I got to ask the second question posed to McGwire, in which he addressed the issue of nearly having missed first base on his home run trot.

Covering the McGwire/Sosa battle in 1998 provided some of the biggest thrills I've ever had as a broadcaster. I ran into Bruce Springsteen who had brought his son to the Busch Stadium press box to witness American sports history in the making. And I stood next to Bob Costas when Big Mac chalked up numbers 69 and 70 on the final day of the season.

Nobody was having a more interesting summer than "The Sportsmonster," Steve Schlanger. In addition to his co-hosting and sports duties on the morning show, he'd landed the prestigious substitute position for Jack Buck on the Cardinals road game broadcasts. Unfortunately, Steve's agent convinced him that Steve needed to quit our show and dedicate his full attention to pursuing more sports play-by-play opportunities. But when Steve Brill caught wind of Schlanger's intent to resign, he read him the riot act. Brill felt Steve's timing was questionable and that his absence would seriously hurt the show at a time when it counted most.

But Brill went a step further with Schlanger in order to get him to stay on. Brill had absolutely had it with the play-by-play man for the football Rams, Gary Bender, and had no intention of renewing Bender's contract after the 1998 season. Bender was a born-again pain in the ass whose screaming matches during the regular Monday morning conference calls with the Rams' production crew had become legendary. (Of the many stories that swirled about Bender, my favorite involves a road trip to Atlanta during which Bender had torn his pants and, later, accidentally squirted mustard on his tie. On the return flight to St. Louis, Bender was complaining to Coach Vermeil about what a rotten day he'd had. Bender was self-absorbed to such a degree that he lost sight of the fact the man he was complaining to had just had his team blown out by over forty points!)

Brill made a deal with Schlanger. If Steve would agree to stay on as co-host of "J.C. and The Breakfast Club," Brill would name Schlanger as the new play-by-play man the following year. Schlanger's agent advised him to take the deal.

In late September we took the show to Milwaukee for a promotion we called "Mac and Cheese," and set up in the County Stadium press box for a special Saturday afternoon broadcast. During the show we learned that Allen Barklage had been seriously injured in a helicopter crash near Parks Airport in Cahokia, Illinois. As the show went on, not knowing his injuries would prove fatal, I recalled the many times I flew with him, and how everyone considered him the best in the business.

It was now the fall of 1998, and I was on an incredible hot streak. I felt I was doing the best work of my career, and we were getting a steady stream of top-notch performers, entertainers and celebrities on the show. But to get most of this material, I had to be in L.A., New York, Milwaukee and Chicago for a total of seven consecutive weekends. I was drained, and I really missed having Karen around to balance the load. In addition, Program Director Steve Brill was feeding me sporadic reports about the general manager's unhappiness with the show. Evidently, although the GM liked the interviews, he didn't appear to like much else; nor was he *at all* comfortable with the idea of regular complaint calls from listeners. Overall, the new company seemed to be treating all of us with a decidedly "move-over-stupid-we'll show-you-how-to-do-it" attitude, blissfully unaware of how hard we all had been fighting to keep the place afloat. We were being treated like a bunch of losers and we resented the hell out of it. When Brill told me the new company was conducting a very expensive market analysis, we realized the fate of the show—and of the station—were on the line.

KSD's studios occupied the second floor of the Pine Street building, with the sales and managerial department residing three floors above. But now with the massive rehabilitation of the second floor underway, employees were being scattered about the building. I realized my plan to impress the new owners might be falling flat when I was informed that my office was being temporarily relocated to an abandoned corner, deep in the recesses of the bottom floor. I would be completely cut off from the rest of the station. It was a hostile move on their part, and a humiliating experience for me. (Except for the fact I wasn't clinging to a red stapler, I really *had* become "Milton" from *Office Space*.)

In an attempt to dazzle our new owners with material and interviews, I spent the next six consecutive weekends on the road. I returned from my final trip at eleven o'clock on a Sunday night totally exhausted. The following day was to be the first in my new, sequestered office. When I arrived at 5 a.m. I found everything had been moved in, but none of my equipment, computers or phones had been set up or connected. I felt as if someone had punched me in the stomach.

I went upstairs to the studio, part depressed, part angry, part disoriented. A mealy-mouthed caller, who had been trying to cause friction between our afternoon host, "The Smash," and me, started jawing with me on the air when it just slipped out. I used the "f" word.

KSD's management seized the opportunity. My suspension for the rest of the week was front-page news in the *Post-Dispatch*. I had just handed my detractors—both inside and outside the station—the ammunition they'd been waiting for.

When I returned to work, I addressed the situation on the air. By its own account, the station had received fewer than twenty complaint calls about my slip. I suggested our listeners e-mail, fax or write what they thought about the situation and about the show in general. Within three days I had over 1,700 pieces of correspondence to lay in front of the general manager's door.

On November 19, 1998, I returned to my office after the show. There, Steve Brill informed me the company had decided to take KSD in a completely new direction and I was being pulled off the air, effective immediately. I finished emptying out my office around eleven that night.

I learned later that, three hours after KSD's new management had pulled the plug on the show, the ratings for October were released. "J.C. and The Breakfast Club" had vaulted all the way into second place in our target demographic of 25- to 54-year-old adults.

We had won the battle but lost the war.

A few weeks later I entered the KMOV building at One Memorial Drive to prepare an interview I'd done with Gwyneth Paltrow for the ten o'clock news. But the piece never made it on the air. Instead, news director, Steve Hammel, informed me budget cuts were forcing him to eliminate the entertainment department at the station. "I wish I had an entire newsroom full of reporters who could ask a question like you," he said, as we shook hands goodbye.

Ninety days earlier I had been sitting in front of television cameras in Chicago interviewing Tom Hanks. It had been only weeks since a crowd of forty thousand had been screaming my name as I co-hosted the Planet Hollywood grand opening on Laclede's Landing.

Now I had nothing.

Postscripts: *I later learned my salary was over $100,000 more per year than the station's new management intended to pay.*

The following week, during a Blues' pre-game show on KMOX, a microphone was left on after a technical mistake, and the "f" word was broadcast. There was no mention of the incident in the media.

Six weeks later, KSD changed its format. Mark Klose was gone, followed by Steve Brill, then Schlanger. The new management did not recognize Steve Brill's Rams deal he had made for Schlanger.

Brand new, state-of-the-art, digital broadcast equipment worth hundreds of thousands of dollars was installed throughout the facility.

I also learned one of our listeners had sent a tape of my annual "Opening Day" show to his friend who works as the official archivist at the Major League Baseball Hall of Fame in Cooperstown, New York. In a letter, I was informed that show had been added to their library of archived material.

"That's my main problem. When I think about myself, it's as a junior in high school. It's time to stop."
—Columnist Bob Greene

Chapter 33

It wasn't a very enjoyable Christmas at our house that year. No matter how much explaining you try to do about the complicated process that determines the fate of a high-profile radio personality, even family and friends are often more affected by the overriding public perception that you just messed up and got fired.

To add to this dismal state of affairs, in a six-month period, Allen Barklage was killed in a crash, my pal Doug Wickenheiser of the St. Louis Blues lost his battle with cancer, and movie critic Gene Siskel, a man I admired greatly, had passed away suddenly.

I got rid of my Chicago-based agent when I realized how little she had done for me, and flew to Washington to meet with another agent, whom I subsequently hired. In the six months immediately following my departure from KSD, a half dozen stations talked seriously with me about coming to work for them. Each time the deal fizzled.

The unfathomable happened next.

On April 16, 1999, Laura informed me she was filing for divorce.

My world went black.

I'd been a good husband, a doting father and, even with the employment interruptions, a rock-solid provider. My parents had been married for fifty-three years, and it never occurred to me that my marriage would be any different. I tried every approach, every emotion, every method, and every conceivable idea to open the lines of communication. The more I tried, it seemed, the worse things got.

I could try to tell you all the things that went through my mind in those first few weeks after Laura dropped her bomb, but I have little or no recollection of anything. Of course, now I had at least two major problems: My family had collapsed, and I needed a job. In fact, I thought if I could get working again it might stabilize my situation with Laura and things might have a chance to improve. I was approached by one of St. Louis' largest investment firms. I marked June 11—the date the training program began—as the deadline for making a final decision about my future and, possibly, for starting a new career.

Instead, though discussions with two stations reached a dead end, I signed on with AM talker, KTRS. Paired with my old friend Wendy Wiese and Hall of Famer Dan Dierdorf, I was being brought in, ostensibly, to reorganize their systems. (Or, to put it in more blunt terms, teach all of that high-priced talent how to do a morning radio show.) Everyone in the room was very talented, each individual funny in his or her own way, but there was no chemistry among the group. This lack of cohesiveness was reflected in the show's miserable ratings in every category, with the exception of the dreaded "55-to-death" crowd.

The move to KTRS also put Frank O. Pinion and I back in the same building. We had a long conversation the first week I was there, and I came away feeling that maybe, just maybe, we now had the foundation for a reasonable working relationship.

A month later he was talking me down again.

Two months later, after every single promise made to me had been broken by the station's manager, I exited KTRS. Frank's attacks increased. Kevin Slaten joined in. A year later, Slaten would be fired, Dierdorf would quit, and Wendy would ask to be released from her contract.

Then, a real heartbreaker. I found out from a former KMOV executive that the producer of Siskel and Ebert's television show had been looking at me for a possible shot at co-hosting with Roger Ebert during the year-long period when they were rotating guest talent. When they learned I'd lost my affiliation with Channel Four, they never pursued the idea any further.

Because of an enormous, pending merger that involved over a half dozen of St. Louis' most-recognizable stations, virtually the entire market was locked up. Even the stations not involved in the huge transaction still went, essentially, into a holding pattern, as most of the radio community seemed to be holding its collective breath. Virtually *every* station in St. Louis had either been sold or involved in a merger in the past five years, and everyone knew the shuffle wasn't over. It didn't help my situation that there was a glut of cheap, available talent.

But an interesting scenario had been slowly developing that involved Jacor, the gargantuan company that had pulled the plug on our show at KSD eighteen months prior. They had merged with yet another corporation, new people were overseeing their St. Louis properties, and I'd been hearing from pals who were still with the station—my former producer, John-John Canavera, and marketing director, Mark Dickinson—that some very complimentary things were being said about me. A meeting was arranged between KSD, Z107, KLOU operations manager, Mike Wheeler, and me while I was still working at KTRS. By the time the new year arrived, we were communicating regularly.

I was just beginning to fumble my way through the process of starting my new life as a single parent. Making the transition from family man with two kids, a wife, a cat, a dog and a 3800-square-foot home to a 1200-square-foot, two-bedroom condo by myself wasn't easy or pleasant, and I'd already had more time to reflect than any one person requires.

With the invaluable assistance of pal Everett Marshall, I began issuing a weekly newsletter I called "JC MAIL." It consisted of all the things I would have been saying had I been on the air, and I sent it to all the listeners who had sent letters of support to KSD's general manager in the weeks before they yanked the show. Word spread quickly and the list of subscribers grew exponentially. If you were one of the hundreds of people who communicated with me during that period, you should know it was your messages of encouragement, appreciation and hope that kept me going during what was the most difficult time of my life. I will never forget it.

I'd made several unsuccessful attempts to contact Karen Kelly, who had left the radio business for the retail industry. Finally, in the spring of 2000, Karen agreed it was better to focus on our seven years of friendship rather than our seven weeks of acrimony. After a few get-togethers (during which I assumed the blame for everything that had happened), one day Karen's smile suddenly returned. I had my best friend back.

Shortly thereafter, I accepted the morning show at KLOU. The plan was to move the Rams over from KSD, and to build a station around me in the morning and "Smash" in the afternoon.

I had no idea Karen had the slightest notion of returning to broadcasting. So, a month or so later when I asked her about it, I was psychologically prepared for her to say no. I was stunned when she said "yes."

The final week of March of the year 2000, everything old was new again. "J.C. and The Breakfast Club" with Karen Kelly, Steve Schlanger and Eric Mink debuted on 103.3 KLOU. You wouldn't have known we'd spent a single day apart.

Postscript: *I learned during our bitter custody battle that Laura was planning to marry her college sweetheart soon after our divorce was final. Although she is no longer my wife, Laura will always be the mother of my two daughters.*

"Be calm and peaceful in your life so that you may be wild and dangerous in your art."

—Novelist Gustave Flaubert

Chapter 34

M y clock radio goes off each weekday morning at 4:15. That's followed by a back-up alarm at 4:20. I shower, shave, brush and flush and arrive at the station around 5 a.m. Anybody who ever says you get "used to the schedule after awhile" is a liar. In truth, it's a lifestyle that requires an incredible amount of discipline and which keeps one permanently out of step with the rest of the world.

When the show ends around 9:30, Karen and I immediately retreat to the medium-sized, powder-blue office we share to begin preparing, not only for the next days' show, but often for shows, contests, promotions and other activities as much as a month or two down the road. Ninety-eight percent of the time we work straight through lunch, which usually allows us to get out before 2 p.m. On occasion I'll have a 10 a.m. screening I'll have to run to, which serves to further complicate things.

The unique custody arrangement I fought so hard for allows me to pick up my daughters from school each afternoon. After I drop them off with their mother around six, I'll spend several hours scanning my five-hundred-plus channels of satellite television, as well as various Internet sites and my own, massive cache of archived tapes, books and clippings to gather material for upcoming shows. At least two nights a week I'll attend movie screenings, but I still seem to find time to play back the "CBS Evening News," *Entertainment Tonight,* the *Late Show with David Letterman*, the *Late Late Show with Craig Kilborn* and *Politically Incorrect with Bill Maher.* I never get enough sleep.

From the moment I wake up, I begin worrying about what I'm going to say and what we're going to do on the air that day. Unlike so many others, ours is a program with an imposing conscience. Which means, in attempting to construct a show each day, we often struggle with the age-old question of what to provide. Should we give the listeners what they want, or what we think they should have? On most days, things land somewhere in the middle.

Electronic media bares little resemblance to the field I entered all those years ago. It's not going to change back, either.

People responsible for shows and tabloids that attack, ridicule and provoke celebrities continue to be among my least favorite people on the planet. The Mike Walkers of the world, who routinely cast aspersions on the collective character and credibility of Hollywood stars, lose what little credibility they have when their shows feature everything from numerologists to Internet goofs. I wish they'd actually show the garbage-sifting that really typifies the level on which they operate.

Unfortunately, tremors from this national trend have been felt on a local level, too. The over-abundance of under-employed traffic reporters, interns, and other entities occupying a spot near the bottom of the broadcasting food chain seem to be generating the lion's share of activity on the Internet, the latest vehicle for the mass distribution of industry poison. At any given time I can dial up any number of radio-related, local websites and read the rantings of nameless, faceless broadcast riff-raff whose work ranges from "amateurish" to "libelous."

Next time you find yourself engaging in gossip, try to remember its definition: "Idle talk or rumor about the private affairs of others." Gossip kills.

If I had to leave St. Louis today, of all the events, celebrity interviews, controversy and vitriol generated over the entire sixteen-plus years, the one thing I believe I would remember most is an episode that happened on the air in 1988.

The Food and Cash Salvation Bash was only in its second year of existence and we still didn't have a sense for how big the thing could get, or how this event was connecting with our audience. As we had done the year before, we went on the air at six in the morning from the West County shopping center, where we would stay for the next thirty consecutive hours. Traditionally at the mall, there was a period of low activity around the dinner hour before things picked up again with the evening shopping crowd. All day long people had come in droves, donating bags, boxes and even skids full of canned goods. About 5:30

that evening, a man dressed in work clothes approached the stage. From the looks of him, he'd had a much harder day at work than I had and, when he handed me a thick, white envelope, I noticed the dirt from his hands had left smudges all over it. Then, he turned and walked away.

In those days it was not at all uncommon for fans to hand me letters, drawings, photos and an occasional manifesto, so I didn't even open it right away. When I did, I found nearly two hundred dollars in cash. After examining the envelope, it was clear this fellow had worked at some sort of dirty, demanding job all day, then cashed his paycheck and brought it straight to me.

Sometimes this job can be very humbling.

I thank the people of St. Louis who have supported me. You've enriched my life. Your kindness, intelligence and humor continually blow me away. I thank the people of St. Louis who haven't supported me, too. You've kept me honest.

A few updates.

Jack Buck now speaks to me. I enjoy that.

I'm back on friendly terms with the people at Emmis Broadcasting and, specifically, KSHE. As both sides have gotten older and wiser it may be that we've come to appreciate just how incredible our time was together.

I'm told Thomas Crone and Richard Byrne, partners in character assassination as colleagues at the *Riverfront Times*, had a serious falling out and no longer speak. At last check, Crone fronts for the civic group, "Metropolis." Byrne left the country.

Frank Absher, one of the great, "Professional J.C. Corcoran Haters," who, for years, masqueraded as a "consultant" and "media critic," now refers to himself as "KMOX's Official Historian."

One half of Steve & D.C. recently contacted me about the possibility of burying the hatchet. While I was intrigued by the gesture, the whole idea would have seemed more convincing had the proposal come with the promise that the use of my daughter's name be permanently discontinued.

And KMOX continues to exert enormous amounts of energy trying to stop, roadblock, interfere and, in many other ways, screw with me on what's become almost a daily basis. Instead of engaging in cheap shots, here's an idea: Why not give it your best shot while I give it my best shot and let's see what happens. Or is that what you're afraid of?

Sometimes I'm afraid my years of yelling and screaming about St. Louis' backward thinking seems to have done little good. I find it pathetic that a market this size doesn't have a full-time movie and entertainment critic on television. It's this type of absence, I believe, that gives St. Louis its reputation. In the meantime, as you read or watch movie reviews, remember there's a huge difference between "intelligence" and "judgment."

Thanks to Larry Lujack and Bob Sirott. I've been able to achieve what I've achieved in this business because of you. And thanks to everyone who ever hired me, particularly John Beck and Merrell Hansen. I put you through heaven and hell but at least it wasn't boring.

What a long, strange trip it's been. I've wrestled a bear, sat in a dunk tank, done shows from a Winnebago for a week and from a blimp over the city. I've flown with Allen under the Eads Bridge and over the Arch. I've gotten to do shows from Moscow and from the temple of sound known as Abbey Road. I've met and hung out with my heroes. One of the great thrills of my career occurred when, in 1993, our staff arranged to have Bob Costas sit in with me on the air for two hours at the Bowling Hall of Fame during a surprise birthday party for me.

It was never supposed to be about *me*. I tried to bring some intelligence and dignity to FM morning radio while still being a goof. Sometimes it worked. Sometimes it didn't. It's still that way. But the vilification I've received in some circles was never supposed to happen. You weren't supposed to take a lot of this stuff seriously. I wanted to be judged by the work, and I believe the work has been, on balance, good. Many of my colleagues give nothing back. I always have.

I'm never going to get the gold watch, the Lifetime Achievement Award or Man of the Year honors. I know that now.

An odd thing happened when the dust had settled following the startling professional and personal events of 1998 and 1999. Instead of becoming bitter and withdrawn, I began to count my blessings. I know, from the many stories of hardship, tragedy, joy and triumph you've shared with me over the years, that we've done the one thing I believe we were all put here to do. We've connected.

In the meantime, we've beaten this one to death. Have a good one. See 'ya later. Bye.